Think and Act on Business Ethics

A RADICAL CAPITALIST VIEW

Barry A. Liebling

Alert Mind Publishing, LLC
New York City

Alert Mind Publishing, LLC
Box 8073
New York, New York 10150
(212) 688-2468
AlertMindPublishing.com

ISBN 1-932877-02-9

Library Of Congress Control Number: 2004092323

Cover design and interior layout by BudgetBookDesign.com.

CONTENTS

PART ONE
SETTING THE STAGE

PART TWO
RADICAL CAPITALIST ETHICS

Preface

WHY I WROTE THE BOOK

My ambition is to have a positive impact on the way you think about business ethics and how you act in the business world. If I succeed, you will be convinced that Radical Capitalist ethics are essentially correct, and you will approach ethical problems in business with the tools to give you confidence that you can solve them.

I have been an observer and participant in arguments about business ethics for a long time—at least since my high school days. Typically the "good guys"—those who are sympathetic to the ideals of Capitalism—have strong attitudes about the issue and do not hesitate to declare that their position is right and their opponents are mistaken. However, seldom does the debate change anyone's mind.

The problem is that while many advocates of Capitalism are quick to announce their conclusions on issues relating to business ethics, they are at a loss when it comes to explaining the underlying bases for their judgments. They know where they stand, but they cannot articulate exactly what justifies their stance.

The solution to the problem is to step back and systematically consider the principles that apply.

My mission in writing this book is to identify and explain the principles that support the Radical Capitalist view of business ethics. I am outlining a systematic, ethical basis for those who are favorably disposed toward Capitalism. My objective is to provide my readers with a framework that will help them to evaluate and plan their own actions.

Furthermore, I intend to give my readers the means to explain themselves so that those who are not yet enamored with Capitalism will come to recognize it as the morally correct way.

DISCLAIMERS

This book presents my philosophical view of how to think and act on business ethics. It is not about the law, nor is it intended to furnish the reader with legal advice. What is lawful, or against the law, varies across localities and frequently changes. I advise the reader to use authoritative sources—not this book—to gauge what is permissible or not permissible according to the laws that apply to where you live.

There are numerous examples of business actions in this book where I mention the names of specific individuals and specific companies. All of the names are for illustrative purposes only. The identities of persons and businesses are fabricated. Any correspondence between the names of my made-up people and companies, and real people and companies, is strictly coincidental.

ACKNOWLEDGMENTS

I take full responsibility for the content of this book. At the same time I recognize that the quality of the manuscript has been enhanced by the critical scrutiny of several of my colleagues. I want to specifically thank Joanne Altman, Patricia Aponte, Wendy Lubin, Lee M. Pierson, and Marilyn Seiler for their helpful, intelligent comments on early drafts of the book.

PART ONE

SETTING THE STAGE

1

BENEFITS AND DOMAIN

WHAT THIS BOOK CAN DO FOR YOU

Let us begin with the bottom line. This book is written for readers who resonate to the ideals of Capitalism. If you have a strong sense that you legitimately own your life, that it is right for you to plan and manage your life for your own sake and for your own happiness, that productive work is the right way to achieve your goals, and that human rights are universal—this book will be useful to you. It is designed to help you in three ways.

Succeed With Radical Capitalist Ethics

Adhering to the principles of Radical Capitalist ethics is both the right thing to do and is the path to material success. While the mistaken belief that ethics and business success are antithetical to one another is common, this book will explain how acting ethically lays the groundwork for achievement. It will show you how to recognize what is morally right, why it is right, and how you should act. When you understand the principles and apply them correctly your prosperity will be enhanced.

Help Others To Understand

Even if you know how to act ethically yourself, it can be a challenge to get the message out to others. This book will give you the tools to explain to your coworkers, employees, employers, suppliers, customers, and any outside observers exactly what the correct principles of business ethics are and how they should be applied. It will help you acquire the skills to be persuasive and to show others the ethically correct way to act in the business world.

Defend Yourself Against Capitalism's Foes

There is no shortage of interventionist critics with antipathy towards Capitalism who routinely smear it and falsely accuse Capitalism as inherently unethical. You may feel that the onslaught of attacks against Capitalism are wrong, that Capitalism is the proper moral economic-political system, yet be unable to argue effectively against them. This book will give you intellectual ammunition to rebut the foes of Capitalism. Once you understand the principles of business ethics you will be in a position to point out exactly why Capitalism is correct and how the critics are mistaken. You will develop an immunity, based on your understanding of what really counts as right or wrong, to resist perverse social pressures and to stay on the proper course.

Of course, not all readers will come to this book favorably disposed to Radical Capitalism. As of this writing, the Radical Capitalist orientation is understood and embraced by a minority of people in business—people who are perhaps the vanguard of a better world. If you are skeptical of the individualist view and its applications to business and ethics, perhaps this book might stimulate you to think about the issues in a different way. It is my intention that some readers—who start out less than enthusiastic about the philosophy that supports laissez-fare economics—might be convinced to change their orientation—recognizing and appreciating the moral validity of Radical Capitalism.

THE ARENA

The domain where Radical Capitalist ethics applies is vast. People are engaging in business activities nearly everywhere you look.

Almost everyone is directly involved in business, usually playing several roles at once. Most people are, or have been, employees of business concerns—engaged in activities such as producing, marketing, selling, purchasing, or distributing goods and services. Many are owners or investors of business ventures. Nearly all people are consumers of the fruits of businesses. You spend your money, and you intend to obtain valuable products. Or, someone else spends money and presents you with the goods.

Even as people are participating in the world of business ubiquitously, they are also making moral judgments—or hearing moral judgments pronounced—about business. A company is praised or condemned for the quality of the products it sells, for its marketing and advertising, for its policies toward its employees, and for its overall "corporate culture." Similarly, particular employees of companies are occasionally honored for adhering to "high moral standards" on their jobs and, conversely, are sometimes condemned for violating particular ethical codes.

While moral pronouncements are being made all the time about business practices, there are widely varying, incompatible views about the standards that should be used in differentiating actions that are ethical from those that are not. This is not surprising since people do not typically share—or even articulate—the assumptions underlying their judgments of what is morally right and morally wrong. It is the underlying assumptions—made explicit or not—that define an ethical system.

Is a software company on shaky moral ground if it becomes fabulously successful and manages to obtain more than 90 per cent of the sales in its market? Is the chief executive of a large automobile company that is not profitable justified in seeking a government bailout? Exactly what does an advertisement have to disclose about a product to assure that the commercial is ethical? What bargaining tactics are permissible, or not permissible, when you attempt to buy something from your neighbor? The methods you use to answer these questions are grounded in your system of ethics—what you mean by "moral" and "not moral."

And it matters tremendously what your ethical system is. If it is conceptualized and formulated correctly, your ethics are your guide to help you realize your human potential. Conversely, a mistaken code of ethics is corrupting and is an obstacle to your genuine success.

False codes of ethics are expounded frequently and loudly—especially in matters that relate to business. A common and highly insidious misconception is the assertion that success in business is inherently at odds with ethics. One often hears sneering clichés such as "You can be successful or moral, but not both," "'Business ethics' is a contradiction of terms," or "You have to decide whether you want to 'do well,' or you want to 'do good.'"

In their uncritical acceptance of the spurious dichotomy—success or morality—some "pragmatic" commentators have suggested that the course to take is to "balance" business interests with ethics. You cannot really have it both ways, they say. If you want to be successful and morally good you have to find a "middle ground" where business interests are compromised to make room for ethics—even as ethics are "adjusted downward" to accommodate the needs of business.

While the fallacy of the "do well or do good" alternative is routinely taken as a truism, it should be soundly rejected. Business success and ethics, properly understood, are in concert with one another. Being ethical is the necessary condition for achieving authentic success in business. Conversely, ethical breaches are debasing to all concerned and are inevitably damaging to those who do the wrong thing.

In this book I am naming the ethical orientation that supports business success "Radical Capitalist" ethics. The term is meant to convey an uncompromising endorsement of pure *laissez-faire* Capitalism. This refers to a social system where individual rights—

including property rights—are recognized, all property is privately owned, and there is a separation of economics and state. Of course, no major country has a system of pure *laissez-faire* capitalism in place. Even the United States, the freest country in the world, has a "mixed economy" where elements of Capitalism are mixed with interventions, controls, regulations, and government enterprises that are in opposition to the Radical Capitalist vision.

So, who qualifies as a Radical Capitalist? I am using "Radical Capitalism" to refer to a constellation of beliefs, opinions, and attitudes about the way society ought to be. A Radical Capitalist is a person who considers the underlying principles of Capitalism to be correct. This person has a sense of life that resonates to the ideal of each individual being free—and encouraged—to live his or her own life as an end in itself, according to his or her own plans with productive achievement and personal happiness as appropriate, moral goals.

Notice that my view of who qualifies as a Radical Capitalist focuses on a person's mindset, not physical—or fiscal—assets. This means that a man or woman with the right attitude—but without large sums of money, not owning substantial amounts of property, not having a position of authority in a large business enterprise—would be counted as a Radical Capitalist. This man or woman qualifies providing that he or she has the Capitalist way of looking at, interpreting, and acting in the world—embracing individualism and rationality.

Conversely, a wealthy man or woman, with substantial assets, who may be running a business enterprise is certainly not a Radical Capitalist—or any kind of authentic Capitalist—if he or she is inimical to the individualistic world-view. It is common to observe wealthy people, who are regarded as "captains of industry" to be supporters and advocates of economic interventionism, government sponsored welfare, socialism, state planning, and other policies that are the antithesis of Capitalism. While these people may be rich and powerful, they should not be mistaken for Capitalists. Instead, they should be recognized as rich people who are yearning for a state-controlled, public-sector-dominated economy.

2

RATIONAL INDIVIDUALISM

The premises underlying Radical Capitalist ethics are derived from a rational individualist orientation. For a full, detailed explanation of the philosophy and reasoning supporting this stance I refer interested readers to Ayn Rand's essays "The Objectivist Ethics" and "Man's Rights" in *The Virtue Of Selfishness* (1964) and "What Is Capitalism?" in *Capitalism: The Unknown Ideal* (1966).

The following presents a brief summary of the main points of Radical Capitalist Ethics.

FUNCTION OF ETHICS

What do ethics do for you? How do you benefit by living ethically? Conversely, in what way is it disadvantageous not to have an appropriate ethical orientation?

"Ethics" refers to a code—a system of principled rules—that a person accepts by choice to guide his or her voluntary decisions. A proper ethical code—based on a correct understanding of the essential nature of human beings—is a tool that permits a person to survive as a human being. By "survive as a human being" I am referring to something much more ambitious than merely breathing, having a heartbeat, eating, and staying warm. "Survival as a human being" implies achieving the conditions that are conducive to the development, self-realization, and happiness of a rational person throughout his or her lifespan.

Applying correct ethical principles consistently in business—and to all aspects of your life—keeps you on track. While the outcomes of business activities, and life in general, are inherently risky and uncertain, ethical actions are the proper path to genuine success. Looking at this from the negative viewpoint, failing to act ethically puts you on the wrong track and separates you from the code that optimizes human survival.

Notice that I am viewing proper ethics as the key to human survival and success. This is in contrast to perversely mistaken ethical positions that assert morality is, in principle, in conflict with your self interest—that morals and personal success must be at odds. This is the false, but commonly heard, notion that the more you are truly ethical the less you seek or achieve personal success, and conversely, the more successful you are the more your morality is suspect.

A person can, and many do, accept a false code of ethics in error. In this case the counterfeit ethics will act as an obstacle to human survival. The code of altruism, a prime example of a mistaken system, is discussed in the next major section.

Besides accepting a false code, people can make a related kind of error—reject the idea of having any ethical system. They live amorally. The consequence of living without an ethical code is that decisions are not based on principles but instead depend on range-of-the-moment expediency, "pragmatic considerations," or whims. An amoral person does not have the concept of what is the moral thing to do. To an amoralist "right" and "wrong" are "social" concepts, and morality is decided by whomever has the power to enforce his will.

ESSENTIAL NATURE OF HUMAN BEINGS

A proper ethical code is based on the correct understanding of the essential nature of human beings.

We human beings have one essential characteristic that permits us to survive—rationality. Human life is the prime value, and rationality is the way to achieve this value. Being rational means to use your senses and perceive the world accurately as it is—looking, listening, feeling, tasting, smelling—and then, to think properly about the world, and to act according to your own best judgment. Being rational at any point in time is the result of conscious choice—you decide to pay attention, to think clearly, and to act appropriately. Conversely, being irrational is the deliberate refusal to perceive and interpret the world as it is, to evade your responsibility to think—to be "stupid on purpose."

To be sure, no person is, or is capable of being, infallible. Even if you sincerely attempt to be rational, there is always a risk that you will not come to the right conclusions. The best people who have the proper attitude toward rationality are frequently making innocent errors. But rational people discover their errors and correct them. By contrast, some of the worst people—those who do not personally value rationality—only rarely think clearly about what they are, will be, or should be doing.

The important point is that rationality is the essential key to human survival—the only road that puts us on the path to living up to our potential as human beings. As such, rationality—and its key derivative productivity—are primary virtues that make human life possible.

THE STANDARD FOR FORMULATING ETHICS

The proper ethical system must recognize human rationality as the prime virtue. In essence, that which promotes human rationality is good and that which undermines rationality is bad.

HOW RATIONALITY RELATES TO FORCE

When we deal with one another we have two fundamental choices—to use persuasion or to use force.

Using persuasion to get what you want from someone is an appeal to that person's rationality. You might say to someone, "If you perform these actions, you can expect these results. If you do this service for me, I will in turn perform a service for you." Using persuasion does not guarantee that you will get your way. The other person may not agree with your reasoning. In fact, after some discussion, you may come to realize that your request is not mutually beneficial, and you will have to come up with a different proposal. Alternatively, your request may be entirely legitimate and beneficial to both parties, but the other person may fail to appreciate the advantages of your proposal, and the deal will not materialize.

Using persuasion gives you a chance to strike the deal that you want, but it does not guarantee it. The person you are trying to persuade may or may not decide to agree with you. For valid, legitimate reasons—or even for foolish reasons—the other person may reject your offer to do business. That you may not get your way is the permanent risk you take when you deal with others using persuasion.

It is noteworthy that outcomes that come about by honest persuasion are always agreeable to both parties. If both participants are forthright, each gets a good deal.

Force is the alternative to persuasion. In its most basic form a person just takes what he wants from someone else. "Give it to me, I want it," followed by a grab is the classic example of using force that every child understands. Using force in a more subtle, but equally reprehensible, manner than the naked grab is coercion—threats of physical harm—"Give it to me or I will hurt you, or I will take even more from you than I am asking, or I will imprison you." More subtle than coercion, but still in the category of using force, is fraud—deliberately attempting to fool, to trick, to mislead another person about what you will take or what you will give in return.

It is important to understand that dealing with people by force is to negate rationality. Rather than counting on a person's best judgment, someone who uses force is denying that person's right to use his judgment and is counting on intimidation or subterfuge to achieve an outcome. Similarly, a person who resorts to force may know that his demands are not reasonable—not likely to come about through a process of honest persuasion. Using force, as opposed to persuasion, in dealing with people is wrong precisely because it attacks rationality—a human being's means of survival.

NATURAL RIGHTS

The rational individualist orientation holds that each person is an end in himself, or herself. Every individual owns and has the legitimate right to his or her own life. Furthermore, no individual may own anyone else's life. Pursuing happiness through rationality and productivity is the morally correct way to act.

Human rights are "natural rights" in the sense that every individual human being possesses these rights, simply by virtue of having the status of human being. They are called "natural" because they do not depend on—or originate from—society, the state, a government, special laws, or leaders.

Natural rights—specifically "life, liberty, property, and the pursuit of happiness"—may not justifiably be violated. They boil down to the freedom of every individual to live his or her life free from physical force, coercion, or fraud perpetrated by other individuals, organizations, governments, societies, or states.

The concept of individual natural rights is profound in its implications. Since the principle is universal, it means that every person is an end in himself or herself. Furthermore, no person may justifiably be sacrificed for anyone else's, or any organization's, interests.

CAPITALISM AND ETHICS

Capitalism, conceptualized correctly, is the social system that recognizes individual human rights. Since coercion—the initiation of force—is a violation of individual rights, business must be a private, voluntary affair. Economic activity should not be government-directed, owned, mandated, or planned. The proper function of government in a Radical Capitalist system is important and is strictly limited—to protect each person's individual rights.

3

COMMON ALTERNATIVE—ALTRUISM

The most popular approach to business ethics is antithetical to the Radical Capitalist orientation. It is the doctrine of altruism.

Altruistic ethics rejects the concept of individual rights, and replaces it with the assertion that you have a duty to serve others that never ends. The altruistic view holds that your business activities are moral only to the extent that someone other than yourself is reaping the benefits. You, by contrast, have no moral claim to the wealth you produce. By right—according to the altruist doctrine—the fruits of your productive activity—your wealth—should be distributed to those who are "in need"—which is never you.

THE MEANING OF "ALTRUISM"

In ordinary common usage "altruism" often has a positive connotation. The term "acting altruistically" suggests to some listeners that the actor is being considerate and kind.

But the doctrine of altruism, articulated in the nineteenth century by the French philosopher Auguste Comte and much admired by many socialist and communist theorists, asserts that it is morally proper to dedicate your entire life to the service of others while taking pains to avoid personal benefit for your efforts. In the business context, altruism implies that your business activities are morally good to the extent that someone other than yourself benefits.

Working in your own interests, for the sake of your own life and happiness is, in the altruistic view, neither virtuous nor moral. The ethical status of actions in your own interest is at best neutral. Sacrificing your interests to others is the path to altruistic virtue. Instead of having a right to your own life and happiness, you have a permanent debt to the "needs" of others. Any activity where you are the recipient of the benefits of your actions is not altruistic. By contrast, subordinating your interests to someone else is altruistic.

To an altruist, making profits are acceptable to the extent that the profits "incentivize" the producer to serve others, but serving others is the main goal of altruism—not producing for one's own benefit.

ADHERENTS OF ALTRUISM IN BUSINESS

You have to look long and hard to find anyone in business who consistently acts according to altruist ethics. In fact, it is not possible to conduct business altruistically—concerned primarily with the welfare of everyone except yourself—and to survive.

What is common, however, is for people—especially critics of business and enemies of Capitalism—to make moral judgments based on some version of altruistic ethics. Altruism, according to its adherents, is the "right way to act," and is also impossible to achieve. The altruist rule is "the less you keep for yourself, the better you are ethically." If you are selling something that other people want to buy, you are on the right moral track if you take pains to assure that you do not reap "excessive profits." If others benefit from your work but you benefit very little, you are—according to the altruist—on moral high ground. If you are intentionally giving more than you are receiving, that is good. If through your efforts in business you benefit others—but gain nothing for yourself and possibly even suffer a loss—you are an exemplar of a person coming close to being ideally "ethically altruistic."

It is noteworthy that the origin of the common cliché that "business ethics" is self-contradictory comes from a tacit acceptance of altruist ethics. Those who repeat the bromide are implicitly recognizing that altruism is incompatible with business.

Among a large proportion of "intellectuals," altruist ethics are mainstream. Journalists, business writers, and university professors are highly likely to espouse some form of the altruistic code of ethics for business.

EXAMPLES OF ALTRUISTIC JUDGMENTS

Here are some familiar examples of the application of altruistic ethics applied to business:

- The business professional who creates a fortune is clever but probably not moral. If he gives a lot of his fortune away, he is a better person—but only if he gives it away to strangers, not members of his family or people who are close to him. If he gives all of his fortune away he has done his moral duty. If he donates his wealth anonymously, taking care to assure that he gets no recognition or credit, he has demonstrated exemplary altruistic behavior.

- The owner of a manufacturing company decides to locate a factory near a small town and hires local residents with the intention of optimizing her company's production. If she is thinking primarily about her own profits, the factory owner will not be seen as doing anything that is morally good. If she publicly proclaims that the reason for moving into the town is to provide the residents with jobs—instead of furthering the company's business interests—it may score altruistic ethical points. If the factory is not productive, the company loses money on the venture, and the owner decides to keep the factory running at a loss—she might be praised by an altruist ethicist for supporting employees even though she is not benefiting herself.

- A company president asserts that the major objective of his business is to serve others—to make products that meet the needs of society. Profits are not his primary objective, he proclaims. Unfortunately, he sighs, in the real world profits are a "necessary evil" that enable his company to perform its duties. An altruist ethicist will give the company president moral credit for apologizing for any profits he and the shareholders of the company make.

CONSEQUENCES OF ALTRUIST ETHICS

It is rare for anyone who runs a business to take altruism to an extreme. Business executives, who see no better ethical alternative, pay lip service to altruism. They learn that the way to get along is to refrain from challenging the "conventional wisdom" that altruism is the path to morality. People usually know that they really want to work in their own interests, and they are not inclined to let altruistic ethics "get in the way of" their business lives. Some pragmatists would say that the way to get along in the real world of business is to say that your motives are altruistic, but you do not have to "really mean it." This attitude is a realization of what many business professionals have been taught in school—ideas are not to be taken seriously. You can, in a superficial, casual way accept the notion that altruist ethics make sense. But deep down you do not sincerely believe in altruism, not literally, not if it interferes too much with your daily life. This, to some people in business, is one of the compromises they agree to make so they can put up an acceptable social front.

Worse than the hypocrisy of pretending to accept the doctrine of altruism is the profanity of genuinely embracing it. If altruism is taken earnestly, everyone else's needs are a permanent claim on your time and effort. You can never pay off your altruist mortgage. The more talented and successful you are, the more you owe. Conversely, the less you have to offer in trade, the more you are entitled to the fruits of someone else's productive work.

ALTRUISM AGAINST INDIVIDUAL RIGHTS

You can recognize the essential correctness of the concept of individual rights or you can cede your rights to the doctrine of altruism. Look at the evidence, think, and discern what is true. Either you legitimately own your own life, have natural rights to the pursuit of your own happiness, or you do not.

Once you understand that you do own your life, the doctrine of altruism is exposed as a sneaky attempt to violate your, and everyone else's, rights. Espousing altruist ethics is the standard tactic used by scoundrels who are trying to disarm and break the spirit of their victims.

ALTRUISM AND BEING NICE

Those who espouse the doctrine of altruism are often able to win arguments by employing an underhanded trick. They set up a false dichotomy—choose between altruism or universal hostility and aggression. Those who are against altruism, they argue, are against being nice.

The intention of the altruist argument is to convince the listener that there are only two possibilities—it is either morally right to be altruistic or morally right to be a brute. They assert that you can either support altruism—everyone's life is the legitimate property of anyone who "needs it"—or you must think that it is acceptable to be habitually nasty, malicious, and to steam-roll over everyone that you can.

Of course, if you think about the altruists' dichotomy, you will see that it is not plausible. Feeling positive regard for other people and projecting sincere benevolence is the way things are supposed to be. The environment that fosters mutual good feelings is one in which everyone's natural individual rights are respected. People get along with one another best when they understand that everyone has legitimate sovereignty over his or her own life and that all dealings must be on the basis of voluntary mutual consent.

The philosophical altruist is stuck with the mistaken notion that someone always has to be sacrificed. The altruist prefers a morality where you are supposed to give your life to others, and the altruist sees the only alternative to self-sacrifice as taking from others. The altruist doctrine does not recognize that the healthy, correct way for people to deal with one another is mutual respect where nobody is sacrificed.

4

THE AMORAL ESCAPE FROM ALTRUISM

A lot of people in business cannot accept an altruistic code of ethics. Many turn to the amoral position which holds that the subject of ethics does not apply to the world of business.

THE CAUSE OF AMORALISM

Frequently, business professionals get queasy when they reflect on the consequences of an altruistic code in business. They know that they cannot embrace a morality that demands that they sacrifice their own interests as a matter of principle. The error that these individuals make is that they do not see any moral alternative to the altruistic doctrine. Consequently, they give up ethics altogether and conclude that morality is a topic that has no place in business.

Some business professionals reject the concept of principled ethics, in business and in daily life, and view it as unreal. To these individuals, it is expedient to drop the idea that there are proper moral behaviors. They want to get on with doing business and not "waste time" thinking about something which they see as ephemeral or fictional.

AMORALISM IN BUSINESS

Amoralists do not act as if they are against ethics or morals. Instead they strive to adapt and behave "pragmatically." They are not interested in the topic of ethics as it applies to business. Instead they focus their energies on being successful, making as much money as they can, any way they can.

To an amoralist, business is the activity of accumulating wealth. A person with this orientation believes it is acceptable to obtain money by hook or by crook. If honest, good work is viewed as a path to money—that might be the course to take. Alternatively, if doing shoddy work, stretching the truth, using deception, or initiating force is seen as lucrative—these policies might be followed.

Amoralists are not necessarily big risk takers. If an activity is against the law, or against company policies, or might be viewed as odious to people who matter—amoralists will be discouraged from doing it. The fear of punishment and reprisals is—according to their own view of the world—what keeps them in check.

THE AMORALIST SELF-IMAGE

People with an amoral orientation in business see themselves as practical, hard-nosed, not bogged down by wasteful musings about what is ethical and what is not.

To an amoral business professional, the practical definition of "right" and "wrong" depends on what is legal and what is not. The best policy is to obey the law. You might get caught and be punished if you do not. If you can give yourself an advantage by finding loopholes in the law—or by evading the law—that might be the way to go. If you think you can influence law makers to obtain special favors for yourself or use government force to cripple the ability of others to compete with you—give it a try.

AMORALISM AND GOVERNMENT

Government is important to an amoralist. It can be a hazard in that you might get punished if you are caught breaking a law. Alternatively, the government can be a tool to be used for your economic advantage. It may be possible, through lobbying and getting laws passed, to get the government to use its monopoly on the use of force for your benefit. The government might bestow economic favors on you that you could never obtain through uncoerced, mutual voluntary trade.

AMORALISM AND ETHICS

To an amoralist, discussions of ethical behavior boil down to power plays. The arguments regarding the moral status of business activities are ploys—word games—to allow some individuals or groups to gain advantages over others.

5

ETHICAL CONSISTENCY

This book is designed to explain Radical Capitalist ethics. I urge you to have a consistent, integrated, systematic understanding of business ethics and to act in accordance with that understanding. Holding a set of rational principles and scrupulously using them is a virtue. Men and women who act this way are correctly labeled as "having integrity."

I recognize that in the world of business many people are not consistent. Their actions can be mercurial. For example, they may apply Radical Capitalist ethics to some situations, later talk like an altruist, and then become resigned to an amoral view.

In popular culture the importance of having integrity, living your life according to a unifying theme, has been discounted. A large proportion of teachers—from elementary schools through graduate schools—admonish their students to be pragmatic, to "go with the flow," to do what is expedient. While they may not know it, they are espousing a philosophy of Pragmatism—a position that advocates being suspicious of principles as such. Frequently, business leaders and public figures boast that they are "not ideological." They are not constrained by any particular system of values.

We live in a world where "having integrity" is not always recognized as being essential. However, the truth is that the courageous path of living according to the principles of Radical Capitalist ethics is both moral and practical.

On the last page of this section is a chart that summarizes the key features of the ethical orientations of Radical Capitalism, Altruism, and Amoralism. It is intended to remind you of the essential correctness of the Radical Capitalist position, and you can use it to explain the position to others.

The next section of the book will describe what Radical Capitalist principles are and how to apply them.

Key Features Of The Three Ethical Orientations			
	Radical Capitalism	**Altruism**	**Amoralism**
Owner Of Your Life	You	Anyone But You	Whoever Can Take It
Main Theme	Rational Self-Interest	Servitude To Others	Expediency
Purpose Of Business	Create Value	Give Away Value	Obtain Value
Intended Trade Outcome	Both Parties Gain	Other Party Gains	Take What You Can
Immoral Action	Violate Anyone's Rights	Work In Your Own Interest	Not Applicable
Function Of Government	Protect Rights	Redistribute Wealth	Tool To Achieve Ends
Who Gets Sacrificed	No One	You For Others' Sake	Others For Your Sake

PART TWO

RADICAL CAPITALIST ETHICS

6

OVERVIEW

I have identified three principles of Radical Capitalist ethics that will help you recognize the extent to which your business activities, or the actions of others, are moral. These principles are tools for sorting out what is ethical from what is not. Once you are proficient at applying them, you will be in a position to recognize when business practices are ethically on the right track and to defend ethical business actions against those who might unjustly condemn them. Conversely, you will be able to discern when and why a business situation is ethically tainted and how to go about setting it right.

The principles of Radical Capitalist ethics are:

- *Create Value.*
- *Act Honestly.*
- *Deal By Mutual Consent.*

Several features of the principles are noteworthy:

BASED ON RATIONALITY

Each of the three principles is derived from the primary human virtue of rationality. This means that while the principles—Create Value, Act Honestly, Deal By Mutual Consent—are focused on somewhat different issues, they are fundamentally connected to one another.

Creating Value is possible because you use your rational faculties to look at your world, to judge what is important, and to devise ways of accomplishing your goals. The policy of Acting Honestly is moral because it counts on your being able to interpret the world accurately and to benefit when other people also see things as they really are. Dealing By Mutual Consent is ethical precisely because it demands that you negotiate with other people by appealing to their rationality—using persuasion—and it condemns the initiation of force as being inimical to rationality.

IDEOLOGICAL

The ideas underlying Radical Capitalist ethics are systematic and principled. As such, they are explicitly ideologically-based—depending on the concepts of rationality, individualism, and capitalism.

Take note that among mainstream political-economic journalists and pundits who fancy themselves as pragmatists, "ideology" is a derogatory term. People in the public eye often go out of their way to boast that they are not ideological—not constrained or tied down by any particular philosophical position. To these pragmatists, labeling someone as "ideologically motivated" is a method of simultaneously delivering an insult and dismissing anything that person has to say.

Of course, pragmatists do not act completely at random. There is almost always some pattern to what they do and what they say. However, by denying that they have any explicit ideology they achieve two furtive objectives. They make it impossible for an outside observer to criticize them for being inconsistent since consistency is not the pragmatist's game. Also, they are able to change course and reverse their opinions at will without feeling the necessity for making excuses.

UNCONVENTIONAL CONSEQUENCES AND JUSTIFICATIONS

I have deliberately taken a fresh look at each principle of Radical Capitalist ethics and have conceptualized it in an extreme, pushed-to-the-limit manner. I expect that as some readers come to recognize the consequences of putting these principles into action they may be startled—hopefully pleasantly so. Frequently people find that taking these principles seriously leads to conclusions they did not anticipate.

I recognize that at first glance, before scrutinizing them carefully, the principles can be seen as clichés—banal truisms that have been uttered so many times that they have lost their impact. However, I suspect that as you come to understand the consequences and justifications for the principles you will see that they are different from the conventional bromides familiar to nearly everyone. For example, in the section "Create Value" you will be shown why "the customer is not always right; in "Act Honestly" you will see why being truthful to others is not the primary consideration; in "Deal By Mutual Consent" you will learn why you have to accept the permanent risk of failure.

Most discussions of business ethics are grounded in social justifications. The main reason why it is either ethical or not ethical to act in a certain way, according to social theorists, is that you are a member of a group, or society, and that you have obligations toward that group. Those who regard business ethics as fundamentally social cannot envision that the subject would apply to someone living alone in isolation.

However, it is important to note that Radical Capitalist ethics are based primarily on how an individual is supposed to act—whether or not there are other people in the vicinity. To be sure, the principle Deal By Mutual Consent only works in a social context since it requires at least two people to apply. But do not lose sight of the fact that Create Value and Act Honestly are valid principles of action for all individuals, whether they are in social situations or living without companions.

REQUIRING THOUGHT AND DELIBERATION

You apply the principles by putting every business activity to three tests—to what extent does your action Create Value, are you Acting Honestly, are you Dealing By Mutual Consent? While asking the questions should become automatic with practice, getting the right answers will always require thought and deliberation. Every business situation has to be evaluated in the correct context. You have to determine what is consequential, what counts as relevant evidence, and how to interpret the facts. There is no mechanical, cookbook-method of avoiding your responsibility to be alert and to think.

7

CREATE VALUE

How To Think About Value

Value—The Foundation

Being productive is a primary human virtue. It is morally right for human beings to make things of value—to create wealth—because this is how humans survive and flourish.

Creating Value is the first principle of Radical Capitalist ethics since it defines the subject. When you think about it, you will see that Creating Value has to be the main purpose of any business. Doing something worthwhile, profiting from your actions, is the primary goal of business activity. Creating Value is a prerequisite for being able to count a business activity as being successful. Conversely, if you fail to Create Value, your business efforts, regardless of how hard you strive, do not lead to genuine success.

This is not to say that your entire life has to be focused exclusively on Creating Value. Any activity has to be judged in its proper context. Everyone experiences countless episodes—acting either alone or in affiliation with others—where there is no intention of Creating Value. A person's life is, and should be, liberally sprinkled with activities that are not productive, including casual recreation, joking and acting silly, idle hobbies, and just plain resting. However, once an activity is defined as "serious business" the aim has to be to Create Value.

Creating Value is a virtue that applies to each individual human being. It is not fundamentally based on social considerations—your relationships with other people. If you were to live alone, in complete isolation, the merit of Creating Value would apply. And the penalty for failing to Create Value would be severe.

Consider the case of Jane Doe, a woman who is marooned on an isolated island. Jane has to Create Value in order to survive. She will have to be productive and take the proper steps in order to assure that she has food, clothing, shelter, and anything else that would make her life possible—and hopefully prosperous. As astute outside observers, we regard Jane as virtuous to the extent that she succeeds in Creating Value for herself. Alternatively, we would be correct in judging her to be foolish if she does not deliberately plan her activities to optimize her success at living on her island.

Of course, in the ordinary real world living in complete isolation is unusual, and associating with other people is the norm. Much of the time, when you Create Value you are making something that you can trade for valuable goods and services that someone else owns. Bear in mind that trading value for value, in the Radical Capitalist view, is a defining process of how people should deal with one another. The alternatives to obtaining values from others by trading values of your own are to be the recipient of other people's gifts or to be a thief.

The negative way of stating the principle Create Value is that you should not intentionally waste your time, direct your activities toward worthless endeavors, squander your life. I am however, deliberately using the positive affirmation—Create Value—because I want to put the main emphasis on what you are supposed to do—not on what you should avoid.

How Value Is Created

You Create Value by producing goods and services that are consistent with your business role. Notice that Creating Value always has a context—what is being done, who is doing it, to whom and for what is it valuable.

The ultimate source of all wealth is a human being using his or her rational mind and acting properly. Someone has to figure out what should be accomplished and how it will be done.

Want to create better shelter? You have to identify what counts as "better shelter" and devise a method for making it. If someone else has already devised the method you can use it to your advantage if you apply it intelligently. Want to make tastier food? You have to invent new recipes which entails deliberate thinking. Even if you are following someone else's recipe, if you want to make good food you have to pay attention to what you are doing. Want to construct a gasoline engine that requires less fuel? You will have to understand the principles of combustion engines and ponder on how to make them more efficient. After the improved combustion engine is developed you build, maintain, and repair it effectively by purposeful action when you are mentally awake.

It is important to understand that Creating Value applies to everyone who has a role in business. It is not limited to innovators, or to people with extraordinarily high levels of intelligence, or to highly paid executives. All competent human beings Create Value, and they all do it by using their rational faculties. For example, consider low paying, entry level jobs—picking fruits and vegetables on a farm, cleaning an apartment, working in a fast-food restaurant. People who take these positions are good workers who are Creating Value to the extent that they are attentive, focused, and use their "common sense" to do their jobs well. Conversely, there are people who are highly paid, with impressive academic credentials, who have prestigious jobs but do not Create Value because they fail to pay attention and apply their minds to achieving their business objectives.

What Counts As Valuable

A product or service is valuable to the extent that it enhances human life—your life. Your intention should be to Create Value for yourself. In some cases you will be the direct consumer of the fruits of your efforts. In other cases you will create products and services that you trade for someone else's products and services.

When you think about Creating Value, the context is key. You have to consider how the goods or services might enhance human life—yours as well as that of your trading partner—and what your official job is.

The main questions you should ask are: on balance, how much does this product or service enhance, or detract from, human life? To what extent should I be involved in providing this product or service?

To help you think about this, here are some examples—not intended to be complete or exhaustive of ways that a product or service might enhance human life:

- Makes it easier or faster to accomplish work.
- Improves the quality of work.
- Improves and maintains health and well-being.
- Is esthetic or entertaining.
- Is informative, educational, enriching, uplifting, instructional.
- Helps people to deal with one another better.
- Makes daily living more comfortable.
- Enhances and promotes pleasure.
- Contributes to living the good life.

Take note that when you are responsible for Creating Value—producing a valuable product or service—you ought to experience a sense of pride. Conversely, if you feel uneasy about the results of your work, or are ashamed of your contribution, that is a sign that you may not be Creating Value. Of course, your feelings of pride or shame are not the last word. When you feel either of these emotions you should take stock of the facts, think things through, and determine whether your work is, in fact, valuable or not.

In all cases the value of a product or service must be discerned in context. It makes no sense to speak of a business activity that has value without considering the setting. It is essential to articulate, "to whom is it valuable and for what purposes."

Take, as an example, the business activity of manufacturing horse-shoes. Is making horseshoes an endeavor that Creates Value? It might be worthwhile if you own a lot of working horses that need to be shod—or if you know that there is a substantial population of horse owners who could benefit by purchasing your horseshoes. Alternatively, you may be living in a setting where horseshoes are of no particular value at all. Perhaps there are not enough horse owners in your world to justify your manufacturing efforts. Of course, horse owners may not be the only people for whom horseshoes are valu-able. Horseshoes do not have to be used on horses. The sport of throwing horseshoes might attract a lot of enthusiasts. Besides being enjoyable, horseshoe-throwing might be a good way to develop hand-eye coordination and to have fun with friends. The point is that you, the person who is considering whether to make horseshoes, has to think about how and in what context they are valuable.

Besides the "to whom and for what" context, you have to take into account the definition of your business role. Whether or not you are Creating Value relates to your role and what your job is. Your job and what you produce have to synchronize.

Consider the case of a sales professional in a real estate company whose official job is to sell or rent commercial buildings and space. When he is at work, all of his activities should support and relate to his main job. The real estate salesman is Creating Value to the extent that he succeeds at selling real estate effectively and efficiently. If he fails to sell, he is not performing well and is not Creating Value.

Suppose the sales professional is simply not good at the real estate business and does not perform his official job well. He loathes the prospect of being fired, so he decides to bake breads, cookies, and pastries—culinary arts are his forte—and give them to his boss and his coworkers in the real estate office. Perhaps they will let him stay. He is ingratiating himself to the other people in the office, but is he Creating Value?

In the context of being a real estate sales professional, the profi-cient baker is not Creating Value. He is engaging in irrelevant activity. But notice that in another context he might be doing a superb job of Creating Value. If he were to go into the baking business, either as an employee or as an entrepreneur, his performance at Creating Value might be distinguished.

Recognizing What Is Really Valuable

Recognizing the extent to which something is valuable requires examination and deliberation. It is something to think about, and the right answer does not come to you automatically. You have to look at the product or service and consider its value in the proper context.

Be careful not to fall for the skeptic's fallacy that you can never be absolutely, infallibly certain of anything. Since you are always subject to error, the skeptic says, you are never in a position to judge. But consider how wrong-headed the skeptic is. Even as you are reading this, you have already gone through a lifetime of routinely making evaluations regarding the worth of a host of products and services. The principle of Create Value requires that you consciously think about what you are doing and make sure it passes reasonable tests of what is worthwhile. And reasonable tests are not arbitrary. There is no escape clause that allows someone to declare on a whim—for no rationale other than wishing—that something is valuable. You have to have good reasons, based on evidence and logic, to conclude that a particular business activity is Creating Value.

Skeptics frequently insinuate that because you are not infallible, you do not have a right to make your own judgments about value. Better, the skeptic might say, to have someone make the judgment for you, take a vote on it, or to avoid judging all together. But the skeptic is wrong. Men and women of integrity know that they will sometimes make honest mistakes, and they take pains to detect and correct them. All people, even the most conscientious, make errors about what is really valuable and what is not. You may have incomplete or incorrect information, or you might take a wrong turn in your reasoning. What is important is that you remain vigilant and strive to discern what is really worthwhile.

Of course, your skill at being able to recognize value will vary according to the subject matter. In general, it is easier to determine what is valuable and what is not when the subject matter is within your own area of proficiency. For example, a professional chemist is in a better position to discern the value of chemical laboratory equipment than is someone with only a passing knowledge of chemistry.

While knowing whether you are or are not Creating Value requires you to think, coming to a correct conclusion is not usually out of your reach. Typically, you can see quickly whether you are on the right track or not. When you have good evidence that you are doing worthwhile work, when you use your good sense to evaluate your performance, it is very likely that you are Creating Value. The proper emotional response to this situation is to be genuinely pleased with that aspect of your job.

Conversely, working people often know or strongly suspect that they are not Creating Value. Some people feel cynical, depressed, discouraged, and complain that they are in a rut. They will confess that they are working "only for the money"—doing what the customer or the boss wants but having no conviction that what they are doing has real value. These people should be alert for better job opportunities.

Customers Are Sometimes Wrong

I am conceptualizing Create Value as an activity that leads to an objectively worthwhile outcome. It is your job to identify, based on the evidence available and your best reasoning, what has value and what does not.

Be aware that taking responsibility for objectively evaluating whether or not you are Creating Value is counter to popular conventional wisdom. It is very common to hear that what is valuable is determined by the market—that a business activity Creates Value to the extent that someone else wants the product or service and is willing to pay for it. This is summarized by the slogan, "the customer is always right."

The widely-accepted, conventional, market value viewpoint suggests that you only have to discover the preferences of your customers—or your boss—to determine how valuable something is. If they are buying—it is valuable, and if they are not buying—it is worthless. Your job as a business professional, according to the market value position, is to give your customers what they want.

By contrast, the objective approach to Create Value recognizes that your customers may be right or may be mistaken about what is really valuable. There are many instances where people are willing to buy products and services that are, in fact, not valuable. Conversely, people frequently fail to recognize the real value of products and services that have tremendous worth.

So, what is the relationship between the objective value of a product or service and the market value? The short answer is that the objective value and the market value are very close to one another if customers are well-informed and carefully evaluate the worth of the product or service. If you "do your homework" you will be able to figure out how valuable something is. By contrast, when customers do not possess the relevant information and do not think accurately about the worth of a product or service, the market value might be substantially different—either higher or lower—than the objective value. Notice how this relates back to rationality. When people have the pertinent facts and act intelligently, they can discern value—otherwise, they are prone to making erroneous judgments.

Consider the example of a purchasing agent, Peter Piper, who is procuring office furniture for his company. He might not have a high opinion of the XYZ brand of office furniture. However, it turns out that XYZ furniture is more durable than other brands. Thus, XYZ furniture can provide a business with more years of service, or can be sold for more money to another business, than competitive brands. Peter Piper mistakenly evaluates the worth of XYZ furniture lower than its objective value and may not be willing to pay a premium for it.

In a related vein, Peter Piper might over-estimate the worth of the QRS brand of furniture. He might not realize that QRS furniture does not accommodate well to new office equipment, has a reputation for being uncomfortable, and will be difficult to sell once it is purchased.

Peter Piper would be likely to change his opinion of XYZ and QRS furniture if he had additional relevant information and considered the matter carefully. The point is that the more Peter knows and the more he thinks about the value of the furniture, the more accurate his judgment will be.

The implications of the objective value concept for marketing and selling is that your customers' desires should not be your first consideration. Potential customers have appetites and preferences for goods and services that may or may not be worthwhile. Your first consideration is to identify products and services that you can deliver that have genuine value. Then, your second task—which is essential to your business success—is to study your customers and determine which of the valuable products and services that you could sell they are most inclined to buy.

Notice that this puts a large responsibility on you, the producer. Your job is not to "give them whatever they want—no matter what." Your mission is to give your customers value, and through honest communication and persuasion help them understand how and why your products are valuable to them. This keeps you "on the hook." You cannot justify producing junk with the excuse that the "customers are asking for it."

When you put your valuable products and services up for sale and your customers recognize the value of what you are selling, you are in a position to do very well in business.

But, what happens if you have genuinely valuable products and services but you are unable to convince customers to buy? Is this unjust? The answer is that it is not unjust. All business enterprises are inherently risky. Customers are, and ought to be, free to accept or reject your offer to do business for any reason—rational or not. More will be said about this in the section on Deal By Mutual Consent.

WHAT YOU SHOULD DO

Here are the steps you take, the questions you should ask and answer, to assure that you are Creating Value.

1. Identify Your Business Role.

Your business role provides the context for what will count as Creating Value.

You have to define exactly what your job is, what business you are in, and what you are officially supposed to do. It is here, in *Identify Your Business Role* and later in *See How Your Role Fits*, that you will come to grips with the issue of conflict of interest. You have to make sure your roles do not conflict with one another. Similarly, you have to assure that your business role is not compromised by a conflicting activity.

It is most likely that you have several business roles. If you are employed you almost certainly have responsibilities in more than one area. For example, at the top of the management hierarchy it is common for a company President to have the job of running the enterprise and also to have responsibilities for "selling" the company to outside investors—persuading them that buying company stocks and bonds are a good investment. Another executive with multiple responsibilities might be the Controller—who could have the task of managing the cash that comes in and out of the company as well as the job of supervising the Director of Human Resources.

Of course, your business roles are not typically limited to working for a company. There are plenty of business tasks that occur outside of the employment setting. Nearly everyone is a consumer—buying goods and services for personal use. As a consumer, you are responsible for a host of activities that might include the maintenance of your household, food selection and preparation, the welfare of children or older adults, or evaluating and selecting entertainment and recreational products.

Among all the business roles that you might play, you have to zoom in on which one, or which ones, are relevant to the situation at hand.

If you determine that you have more than one business role that is relevant, you have to be alert to issues that relate to conflicts of interest. That is, your attempt to perform one role undercuts your ability to do the other. This works against your ability to Create Value.

Sometimes it is not obvious whether two particular business roles will inevitably result in a conflict of interest. An outside observer will see the potential for conflict, will notice that there are incentives that might discourage someone from acting correctly. However, a conscientious business professional will take pains to meet the requirements of each role, will not be corrupted, and will do both jobs well. This type of situation, where a person may or may not have a real conflict of interest depending on his or her attitude and actions, is often called "the appearance of a conflict of interest."

There is no question that scrupulous business professionals routinely resist perverse incentives and do the right thing—performing two roles well—which potentially conflict. At the same time, for some people, having two roles that can conflict, does lead to bad results. They simply cannot do a good job at both tasks.

Often executives who formulate company policies—having a strong desire to keep the employees on track and avoid conflicts of interest—put in rules that forbid employees from taking on roles where there is an "appearance of a conflict of interest."

A classic example of a potential for conflict of interest is the lawyer who might be asked by both the plaintiff and the defendant for legal advice. The lawyer recognizes that working zealously for one of the litigants precludes her from doing a good job for the other. There is no easy way to take both sides and perform well for each client.

You often hear that people who provide financial services are routinely in situations where the potential for conflicts of interest are significant. When your stockbroker makes a commission every time you buy or sell stocks and bonds, the stockbroker may be incentivized to encourage you to trade your securities frequently. The stockbroker's incentives for trading might work against his ability to give you good advice about whether it is to your advantage to trade at all.

In fairness, however, there are many stockbrokers who are able to give good advice to their clients and make commissions on trades at the same time. You, as the client of the stockbroker, have to decide whether you want your broker to give you advice as well as to make commissions on trades. If you want these roles combined you have to take care to select a stockbroker who earns your trust.

Suppose you are an interior designer who advises homeowners on how to remodel kitchens and bathrooms. You might have as part of your full-service package the ability to implement the renovation for your clients, using a contracting company that you partly own. In this scenario there is no apparent conflict of interest in roles since your clients know from the start that you are in the business of giving them complete solutions.

Alternatively, consider the case where you only sell your home-owning clients advice on how to remodel. You do not implement any construction, but you recommend contractors to them who they are free to use or to reject. If your clients do not know that you are part-owner of a kitchen and bathroom contracting firm that you recommend to them, your ability to provide value as an advisor may be tainted.

Finally, consider the case of an apartment rental agent who promises to find an inexpensive apartment for someone who is new to a city. If the broker is also paid a percentage of the rent by the apartment owner, the broker will have conflicting interests. He may have trouble simultaneously finding the best deal for the tenant and getting the most rent he can for the apartment owner.

What should you do if you discover your business roles are in conflict, or potentially in conflict, with one another? Either get rid of one role, or disclose clearly to your customers that you have both roles.

Getting rid of one role is the surest, most straightforward, way to solve the problem. Think back to the lawyer—she knows it is proper to take on one, not both, potential litigant clients. Consider the stockbroker—he may decide to trade equities for a commission or to sell his advice, but not both. Recall the interior designer—he might elect to get rid of his interest in the contracting company.

The alternative to giving up a role is to disclose fully your potentially conflicting roles to your customers. The stockbroker could clearly explain to each customer exactly how he benefits every time an equity is traded. The interior designer could announce to his clients that he has a financial interest in the success of a specific contractor that he often recommends.

2. Define The Product Or Service.

If you are responsible for a product or service, you have to know all the relevant facts about what its elements are. This is a requirement for being able to determine the extent to which the product or service has real value.

You should have good answers to the following types of questions:

- What exactly is being created or is supposed to be created?

- How well does your version of the product or service perform? How does it stack up against alternatives that might be provided by someone else?

- What will you be doing? What actions will you be taking that will cause the product or service to come into being?

- If the product is tangible, what are its characteristics? How will you recognize whether it is made well or made poorly? What are its ingredients? How will it be manufactured? Who will be involved in making it?

- If it is a service, what is supposed to be accomplished? What counts as competent delivery of the service? Where might things go wrong?

- How will the product or service be used? If it is for sale, how will it be sold? How will it be delivered?

3. See How Your Role Fits.

Your business role and the product or service that you are evaluating have to come together. When they mesh properly you are "sticking to your knitting," doing what you are supposed to do, "minding your business."

Ask yourself why you should, in your role, be producing this? Why is it important to your job? If the product or service is executed well, what impact will this have on the success of your business role? If it were not produced well, how would it blemish your record of accomplishments?

You have to determine which of three alternatives applies:

Congruence—the first alternative.
Your role and the product or service fits.
This is where you should be. The business activity supports and enhances what you are supposed to accomplish. Here you are in the appropriate arena, doing what will contribute to your success in your job.

Unrelated—the second alternative.
Your role and the product or service do not connect.
There may be occasions where you consider the product or service in relation to your job and conclude that they are not directly related. If there is no necessary connection, the business activity could be a distraction, a waste of your time, something that diverts you from your real mission of Creating Value.

The business activity might, in fact, have real value in another context. However, it does not support your role. In this case it is really "none of your business."

What should you do if you come to this situation? You can move on and concentrate your efforts on activities that really count. The unrelated activity is someone else's job, and it should not interfere with what is consequential to your job. Alternatively, if you are really interested in the business activity you might decide to change your job and take a position where your official duties include that activity.

Consider the case of the mid-level financial executive who really enjoys entertaining his fellow employees. He spends a lot of his time making the rounds, meeting and greeting, bringing cheer to people, telling jokes, singing songs, exerting sincere efforts to assure that everyone around him is in a good mood and that morale is high. Pleasant and likeable as this man may be, he is not able to be both the "office social director" and competent as a financial executive. A stern supervisor might reprimand this financial executive and warn him to knock it off, get his nose to the grindstone, or face dismissal. The problem is that the financial executive's charm does not have real value in the context of his official job. Perhaps the best way for him to solve his job performance problem is to change careers and do something where he enjoys his duties. He might transfer within the company and work as an employee relations specialist. He might change his vocation radically and become a professional entertainer.

Conflict—the third alternative.
Your role and the product or service clash.
Be careful to avoid taking on business activities that are at odds with your main business role.

Previously we considered conflict of interest where two of your business roles might clash with one another. Here, we are examining the case where you notice that a product or a service that you might provide conflicts with your rationale for doing business.

My advice is not to go there. If you are earnest and sincere about doing a good job, you do not knowingly take on activities that are incompatible with that job.

Here are some examples of products and services that can clash with your main business role:

- You own and run a health food store. Your main mission is to make foods, supplements, and vitamins available to your customers that will help them to be in the best of health. Everything sold in your store has your implicit approval. You know that many of your customers are cigarette smokers. Should you sell cigarettes at your store? No, because selling cigarettes is inconsistent with running a business that is dedicated to improving people's health.

- You manage a local bank, and you distinguish yourself from competing banks by aspiring to be the trusted financial advisor to your customers—giving them the best in banking services. Your marketing efforts emphasize that consumers with accounts at your bank can feel confident that your institution can be trusted to offer high quality products. A representative of a credit card company approaches you and suggests that your bank offer easy-to-get high-interest loans—that would be managed through the credit card company—to checking account customers. In your opinion the credit card loans would not be advantageous to your customers, and you would not personally recommend the financial product. Should you collaborate with the credit card company on this venture? No, because you want to provide value to your banking customers and you have concluded that the loans are, on balance, not a service you would endorse. To offer this product would contradict your claim that you are selling your customers high quality financial services.

- You are a neighborhood locksmith and your main mission is to help your clients maintain a safe, secure environment. At your store you sell a variety of merchandise that includes locks, safes, guardrails, reinforced doors and hinges, and alarms. You have an opportunity to sell lock-picking kits that include instructions on how to open most common locks. Should you include these lock-picking devices in your store inventory? Probably not. Your main job is to help your clients to maintain their personal security. You do not want to get into the business of advising and helping scoundrels who are your clients' adversaries and who aim to get around your security measures.

4. Articulate What Is Valuable.

Once you have established that it is congruent to your role, you should consider the extent to which the business activity has genuine value. Do not lose sight of the fact that Creating Value is the main reason for any business activity. It is your job as the producer to know what you are doing.

The bottom line is that you have to be able to explain how the product or service contributes to human survival and prosperity— your prosperity if it is for your own consumption, your customer's prosperity if you intend to sell it. While this requires some deliberation, it is not unreasonably difficult. You already have a lifetime of experiences where you have categorized products and services as being very valuable, somewhat valuable, slightly valuable, or worthless. Your job is to do it again, in a thoughtful way.

Here are some guidelines on how to proceed. Ask and answer the following kinds of questions:

* What will the end-user—you or your customer—of this product or service gain? What are the main benefits? What makes it worthwhile?

  It is not sufficient to say that your customer wants the product or service and is willing to pay for it. Customers can be mistaken about what has value. To be sure, it is crucially important that your potential customers see the value and have a desire to acquire it, or you will never be able to sell it. But your job of Creating Value is not simply to comply with what is requested of you.

- How are the benefits of this product or service any different or better than if the end-user were to obtain or consume something else? Considering the category of this product or service, what makes it distinctive, advantageous, or more economical?

- If you are—or hypothetically could be—in the target market for this product or service and you know all the relevant facts, would you buy it? If so, why? If not, what reasons would you have for not purchasing it?

- What are the consequences of doing a competent job of delivering the product or service? How much would it matter? Suppose you did a poor job? What difference would this make?

    When it matters a lot whether you do a good job or a poor job, you have evidence that the product or service has higher value. Similarly, if there is little impact whether you are fastidious or slipshod, the business activity is likely to have less value. As an illustration, consider how consequential it is to design headlights properly for an automobile. Contrast that with how much it matters that the lights in the automobile's trunk work well. Each type of light has some value, but it is obvious that the headlights are more valuable than the trunk lights.

- To what extent would you feel proud to be responsible for this product or service? What exactly would make you feel good about it? By contrast, to what extent would you feel uneasy about being responsible for this product or service? What is making you feel uncomfortable?

Having emotional feelings—good or bad—about a business activity is a sign that you should investigate. While your initial impression may be correct or mistaken, it is important to look at the evidence, think things through, and come to a valid conclusion about how valuable the business activity is.

- What are your sources of information in answering these questions? What are the bases of your judgment? If you have relied on outside "experts," what are your grounds for trusting them?

At the end of this exercise you will be in a position to explain both to yourself, and to others, how you are Creating Value—the ways your business activities are designed to result in worthwhile outcomes.

Following are some examples where Creating Value is apparent:

- You are starting a new brand of bottled water. The product is designed to be cleaner, tastier, and less expensive than the leading brands. Furthermore, you will be using a unique easy-to-open container that stacks and stores well in small places.

- You are writing a screenplay for a motion picture. Your intention is to produce a movie that is funny, employs the clever use of language, and has a message that is instructive.

- You will be selling an imported ball point pen that has a graceful design, making it remarkably comfortable to handle. The pen will sell at a lower price than other imported pens of equal quality.

- You will be doing public relations activities for a child care service. The service is distinctive in that the owners have a serious commitment to providing a healthy environment where the children are encouraged both to learn and to have fun.

By contrast, consider examples where the objective of Creating Value is suspect:

- You are starting a new brand of bottled water. The product is bottled in the conventional manner. In order to be certain the water is safe, you intend to add a significant dose of chlorine which—besides reducing the risk of contamination—will also make the water take on a "chemical" smell and taste.

- You are writing a screenplay for a motion picture. You are not personally interested in the subject matter, but you believe that a particular movie producer will pay you to write a script that is primarily concerned with showing car crashes, explosions, and gun battles. You calculate that after you sell this screenplay you will have the resources to do something that is "really interesting."

- You are considering whether to sell an imported ball point pen that, at a glance, looks just like a particular pen marketed by a famous designer. You suspect that potential customers will mistake your imported "knock off" for the designer pen—an error that you believe the manufacturer hopes people will make. You anticipate that some customers will be disappointed with the imported pen and will inadvertently blame the famous designer.

- You are considering taking on a public relations assignment for a child care service. You have met the owner and regard him as a shady character who you would not trust with your own children. Still, you entertain the possibility of taking the assignment and rationalize that the parents who read your glowing press release will probably investigate the child care service assiduously on their own.

5. Consider The Downsides.

You have to consider the downsides, or potential downsides, of the business activity. Here I am talking about dangers, risks, and unwanted consequences.

Be careful to avoid two common errors. The first error is to skip this step altogether. It is a mistake to think that once you show that the business activity has some value you need not worry about liabilities. Just like prudent pedestrians who get in the habit of looking both ways before they cross the street, you should take stock of the liabilities of your business activity as part of the process of judging its net value.

The second error is to be discouraged too easily and give up on your project when you should not. You do not want to be inappropriately alarmed and quit as soon as you identify any downside.

Be aware that all products and services have potential downsides. Anything that can be used can also be misused. A hammer intended for carpentry can be abused to hurt someone—either by imprudent accidents or by deliberate malice. Any food, drink, oral pharmaceutical, or dietary supplement—including water—can be consumed extravagantly or foolishly and might harm the person who ingests it. Even an innocuous book or magazine can inflict annoying and painful paper cuts on careless readers.

Your job is to identify the significant—as opposed to trivial—downsides of the product or service. How do you discriminate between significant and trivial?

The short answer is you have to use your common sense. If the downsides are minor, extremely improbable, easily avoided by nearly anyone who does not have malicious intent—the liabilities are likely to be trivial. Consider the case of a published book that might give the user paper cuts. Ask yourself, "Is the paper distinctively sharper or more perilous than what is used in most other books? Do I expect that the book will get into the hands of people who are accustomed to handling books, who are familiar with the perils of handling crisp paper? Is it sensible to warn buyers and readers that they have to be cautious when they turn the pages, or is it reasonable to expect that the end-users will be book-savvy?" Assuming the book in question is physically an ordinary book intended for a general audience, you can probably dismiss the paper cut hazard as trivial.

What about significant downsides? How can you identify them and what should you do when you find them?

Again, you should ask and answer questions which will reveal the nature and consequences of the downsides of the product or service. It is noteworthy that the solution to the downside is often made obvious when the downside is articulated well. You can change something about the product or service, sell it or communicate about it carefully, or conclude that the product or service is fatally flawed.

Here are some leading questions that will help you understand the downsides:

- Who will be using the product or service, and who will be affected by the end-users?

   Will it be adults or children? Sophisticated professionals or inexperienced novices? People who have a track record of using similar products safely or beginners who do not have a clue about the product category?

- What can go wrong that is due to the design and manufacture of the product itself? What might wear out, fail, malfunction? How can the product be changed to get around these problems?

   Products that are designed to be resistant to accidents are often more valuable. The safety razor—which exposes only a small part of the blade making deep accidental cuts improbable—has advantages over the straight razor. An automobile with two independent braking systems is better than the same car with only one braking system.

- What can go wrong that would be attributable to end-users' lack of knowledge or skill? How can you effectively communicate with end-users to minimize product abuse? How might you identify and deliberately market to end-users who will use the product responsibly?

  Safety instructions and warnings can help end-users avoid danger. For example, aspirin can be bad for people who have stomach sensitivities or are prone to bleeding. Electric fans and heaters should not be used too close to tubs full of water.

  Sharp kitchen knives are intended for adults who have some minimal degree of competence in food preparation—not for small children or for older adults with poor motor coordination. Medical and surgical equipment is deliberately marketed to professionals who are supposed to know how to use it.

  Note well that you should be designing products for people who are striving to be reasonable. You cannot, and should not attempt to, contrive products that are completely "fool-proof" or "malice-proof." People who are deliberately stupid or intentionally villainous will always find a way to express their atrocious nature. There is no cutting instrument, tool, medicine, food, or tangible product that a determined fool cannot corrupt and bring about harm.

- How inherently risky is the category of the product or service?

  Explosives are riskier than furniture polish, and furniture polish is riskier than baseball caps. Trains, planes, and automobiles have more risk than office chairs, coffee tables, and serving trays.

- Within its category, how risky is your specific product or service?

Stainless steel steak knives are riskier than disposable plastic cutlery. Enteric coated aspirin works slower than uncoated aspirin, but it is less likely to cause stomach distress.

What should you do about real liabilities? Find a way to mitigate them. Redesign the product or service. Sell it selectively. Include information that warns end-users and those around them of the downsides and your suggestions on how to minimize problems.

What if the liabilities are significant and you can see no way to mitigate them? There may be no obvious way to fix the problem. This is the point where you should quit—do not engage in that business activity at all. For example, there is nothing you can say about tainted food that will make it acceptable—no one should eat it. Similarly, if you have an inventory of umbrellas that leak and break the first time they are used, the downside of the product precludes the umbrellas from being useful.

6. Calculate The Net Value.

Here you have to determine the extent to which, on balance, the business activity is worth pursuing or not.

In essence you look at the positive value that you anticipate the activity will generate and balance it against the liabilities—especially the liabilities you cannot fix.

When you perform this task competently you will know whether or not you ought to be involved in the business activity, and this knowledge will be based on the evidence available and your best judgment.

Consider an example that illustrates how you might do the calculations:

Jack Sprat is a business professional who wants to buy and run his own company. Two companies are for sale at a price he can afford—a pharmaceutical company that manufactures generic aspirins and a tobacco company that makes generic cigarettes. Jack has to decide between the two companies.

First Jack thinks about the aspirin manufacturer. Aspirin is used extremely widely and has been sold under various brand names for a long time. The positive value of aspirin has been demonstrated clinically. It is one of the most popular analgesics and is useful for treating—among other things—headaches, muscle aches and pains, inflammation, fever, and coronary disease.

And aspirin, like all pharmaceutical products, has downsides and risks. Some of the common well-known liabilities are that it can irritate the gastro-intestinal tract causing distress among those who are sensitive, it can make the blood too thin and promote bleeding, and a small proportion of consumers are allergic to it.

On balance, is aspirin valuable? Is getting into the aspirin business a worthwhile endeavor? The answer is "yes." The assets of the product, the ways in which aspirin contributes to the survival and prosperity of Jack's potential customers, are significant. The downsides of aspirin can be mitigated—and routinely are minimized—by clear instructions about how to use it and warnings about its potential side effects.

Now consider the cigarette company. Tobacco is used by millions of people all over the world, and manufactured cigarettes have been sold for more than one hundred years. The positive value of cigarettes is chiefly recreational. Many smokers report that they enjoy the experience, and it is common for smokers to regard cigarettes as a daily necessity—something they would be reluctant to give up voluntarily.

The downsides of cigarettes are well-documented. Long-term use of cigarettes hurts smokers' health—contributing to heart disease, vascular disease, and cancer. There is some evidence that smokers may be physically harming others with their habit—"passive smoking" might be detrimental to those who are in the vicinity of smokers.

On balance, are cigarettes valuable? Is marketing cigarettes a worthwhile endeavor? Using his best judgment Jack concludes the answer is "no." The downsides of cigarettes do not go away with special warnings. There is no way to be a cigarette smoker who is using the product safely.

I have deliberately constructed the aspirin and cigarette examples to be banal. Readers probably anticipate from the beginning that the aspirin business will turn out to be acceptable while dealing in cigarettes will not. The cases were fabricated to make it easy to see the type of reasoning you should do.

But this line of argument should always be done in context. The relevant landscape could change and cause you to come to different conclusions.

To show how context is always important, let us revisit cigarettes and aspirin. This time, we are looking at these products in a world where the circumstances have changed. New pharmaceuticals with aspirin's benefits may be developed. Researchers may discover significant benefits that can be obtained from cigarettes.

Suppose there were a new anti-inflammatory drug called "Aspirin Not." The chief characteristic of Aspirin Not is that it has all of the benefits of aspirin, but significantly less severe side-effects. Consumers who take Aspirin Not respond as if they consumed aspirin but they are uniformly less likely to suffer any distress. To make this hypothetical example complete, assume that Aspirin Not has gone through extensive clinical trials proving its efficacy and safety, will be made available over-the-counter, and will sell for less money than aspirin.

Now in this new world is it worthwhile to make and market aspirin? Perhaps not. If there were an equally effective, safer, less expensive way of obtaining aspirin's benefits, the downsides of aspirin may, on balance, persuade Jack Sprat not to get into that business.

Back to the cigarettes. Someone may develop a tobacco-based cigarette, New Cigarette, that can be proved to deliver important benefits that go beyond recreation. Perhaps the New Cigarette will markedly increase the intellectual functioning of the smoker. Scientists, writers, or business professionals might be far more productive if they spent one day a month, in isolation, dosing themselves with this novel tobacco product. While the New Cigarette is not safer than conventional cigarettes, its remarkable benefits demand that you take a fresh look in evaluating its worth.

Would it be worthwhile for Jack to buy a business that sells a generic version of New Cigarette? Possibly. If potential users were told of its downsides, if smokers were urged only to consume New Cigarettes in private, it is conceivable that a case could be made that marketing the tobacco product has a net positive value.

8

ACT HONESTLY

How To Think About Honesty

Honesty—Respecting Reality

Honesty is fundamentally important. Acting Honestly is adhering to the policy of recognizing what is real and what is not real and basing your actions according to what is real. Being honest with yourself and with those with whom you do business is an essential part of being committed to rationality—both in yourself and in others.

How does Honesty connect with rationality? You can only be an intelligent agent in the world if you conscientiously separate what is real from what is not. Your important decisions should be grounded on the evidence that is available to you and your clear thinking. This gives you the best possible shot at success. Conversely, basing your decisions on what you know is not real—on lies—is to counterfeit the truth and to condemn yourself to failure.

Of course, there are appropriate times and settings for considering and discussing things that are not real. There are many occasions—inside and outside of business—where it is right for you to let your imagination and dreams run free. Everyone reflects on ways that the world might be different from how it really is. Creating fiction and being entertained by someone else's fiction can be extremely valuable. Following the lives of contrived characters, seeing how they act in various situations and respond to events that are not real—but perhaps could be—can be an esthetic as well as an educational experience. In the world of business, taking time to speculate about possibilities that are not real—new products, improved production methods, novel distribution systems, innovative ways of communicating—can be both enjoyable and instrumental in helping you plan your business activities.

But fictions must be recognized for what they are—fantastic fabrications—and not confused with reality. Sticking to reality when it counts is central to Radical Capitalist ethics.

Being honest with yourself means you conscientiously do your best to learn the truth about issues that are important to your business. This means scrupulously seeking out relevant information and evaluating it thoughtfully. Whatever your business activity is—for example making, maintaining, investigating, distributing, buying, or selling—you should do your best to know what the attributes and benefits—as well as the liabilities and potential dangers—of the activity are.

Having the policy of being honest with yourself does not mean that you are supposed to be—or can be—infallible. Even people who are highly motivated to be truthful, who have an intelligent and meticulous mindset, make mistakes frequently. You may err because of incomplete information or faulty reasoning. But you are on a proper moral course if you sincerely attempt to know the truth, frequently check your conclusions, and correct your inaccuracies as soon as you can.

There is a severe moral problem with deliberate self-deception—also referred to as "evasion." A man or woman who purposely looks away, refuses to see, turns his or her attention from what is important toward something that is inconsequential, willfully refusing to understand—is guilty of evasion. A business professional who "does not want to know," "would rather think about something else," "chooses to be unconcerned with the merits of the business activity" is guilty of running away from an important responsibility.

Acting Honestly, like Creating Value, is a virtue that is grounded in the individual and is not socially based. Even if you live in complete reclusiveness and do not interact with other people, Acting Honestly is essential.

Consider the case of Jane Doe, the woman we met earlier in the section on Create Value, who is alone on an isolated island. Jane must Act Honestly to survive. She has to grasp what is real and consequential in order to assure that she is able to produce her food, clothing, shelter, and other essentials. Jane will not succeed on the island if she confuses her fantasies or wishes with what is really true. For example, Jane must learn quickly and accurately what is real with respect to which animals might be dangerous, which plants are edible and which may be toxic, and how to obtain drinking water. Deliberately evading these important questions—or answering them whimsically by relying on wishes or random guesses when there is reliable evidence available—is failing to Act Honestly and generally leads to disaster.

The social application of Act Honestly is what many people usually think of first when they consider the topic of honesty. When you deal with others and your intentions are benevolent—as opposed to hostile—you should be truthful. In the context of Radical Capitalist ethics, the social meaning of Act Honestly is that whatever you tell your trading partners about your product or service you should believe it to be true, you should have good reasons for believing it is true, and you should craft your communications to be clear to your intended audience. The alternative to Acting Honestly is to be a trickster—attempting to mislead people with whom you are trading.

If you Act Honestly when you deal with others you are counting on their rationality—to be informed, alert, and intelligent. The more they have valid, reliable information about what you are offering, the more they will be able to see the value of doing business with you. When two trading partners are honest with one another they "put their cards on the table" and each is banking on mutual good judgments to come to an acceptable agreement.

By contrast, when someone does not Act Honestly when dealing with others he is counting on the ignorance, gullibility, lack of attention, and foolishness of his victims. The scoundrel who attempts to deceive others and is looking for "suckers" has explicitly rejected the virtue of seeking out trading partners who act rationally.

The conventional rationale for Acting Honestly when you deal with others in business is the principle of reciprocity. It is said that if you are honest in business your potential trading partners will recognize it, will feel comfortable doing business with you, and will likely reciprocate by being honest with you. Conversely, if you are dishonest your reputation will be tainted, others will not trust you, and potential trading partners will avoid you.

While it is true that people will tend to reciprocate, the conventional rationale does not go far enough. It leaves open the possibility that there are some business situations where it is acceptable to eschew honesty for trickery. Someone fixated exclusively on reciprocity might mistakenly believe that if you will never have to do business with a particular customer again, perhaps you can get away with being dishonest.

The Radical Capitalist ethics principle of Act Honestly takes the long-term view. The reputation you deserve, the way others are supposed to judge you, depends on all of your actions. If someone attempts to trade in a dishonest manner, that person is committing a fraud—which is a violation of individual rights. Honesty is not merely the best policy, it is the only acceptable way of doing business with others.

Context And Importance

Acting Honestly has to have a context. The resources you have for investigating and communicating are limited. Among all the issues that might be part of your business environment, you have to differentiate what is important, consequential, and essential from what is not. A wise person focuses on what is important. She devotes attention and time to issues that really matter and puts peripheral subjects on the back burner or ignores them all together. A fool is characterized by the exact opposite policy—finding minutia and marginally relevant topics compelling and wasting time on the unessential without ever getting to what is important.

You have to identify what about your product or service, or the one you are investigating, matters—the attributes that contribute to its value and that might detract from its value.

Consider the example of the man we met previously in Create Value, Jack Sprat, who has recently purchased an aspirin manufacturing company. It is consequential for him to be very well informed on topics such as the chemistry of aspirin, the processes used to make it, the economics of manufacturing and selling aspirin, its pharmacological properties, its clinical applications, and the risks and dangers of packaging, distributing, prescribing, and using aspirin. Not only should he know the relevant questions and answers, he has to be able to communicate effectively about his business with his colleagues, vendors, employees, and potential customers.

 Exactly how much about your company and its products you are supposed to know depends on your role and your relationship with your company. If your relationship is narrowly defined you may only have to know about what impinges on your job. If your official role is central, it behooves you to know a lot more. For example, if your job at a large accounting firm is to manage the company's cafeteria—you had better know all the important facts about your function including food selection, preparation, vendor relations, hygiene and safety procedures, costs of operation, and cafeteria personnel policies. But as the cafeteria manager you are not required to be an expert in accounting.

By contrast, the managing partner of the accounting firm has different responsibilities and a different list of issues that are consequential to his role and appropriate for him to know well. This executive—who has ultimate responsibility for all business units in the firm, including the cafeteria—has primary obligations for knowing the essentials about what the firm is doing for its clients, how the firm is at risk, and how it assures quality control in its auditing work. While the managing partner is supposed to warrant that the cafeteria runs properly, he might be able to meet his obligation by hiring a competent cafeteria manager.

Honesty And Secrets

Acting Honestly requires that whatever you say to your trading part-ners—or potential trading partners—has to be true and you have to say it in a manner calculated to be accurately understood. This does not imply that you are obligated to reveal everything you know to anyone who asks. While you have to be careful to communicate truth-fully and clearly, you have a right to keep some things to yourself.

Suppose you are attempting to sell an ordinary wooden chair to Peter Piper, the purchasing agent we met in Create Value. What must you disclose about the chair?

It is reasonable for you to assume that Peter Piper, a professional purchasing agent, is experienced with ordinary wooden chairs. Consequently, you may only need to show him your chair and tell him your selling price. Peter will use his best judgment and decide whether or not he wants to pay your price.

However, it is possible that there are special characteristics about the chair, not readily apparent to Peter Piper, that set it apart from "ordinary chairs." If you believe that Peter is expecting a conven-tional wooden chair you may need to tell him more about your merchandise to be sure you do not mislead him. For example, perhaps you know that the chair was originally made for a motion picture production company and was constructed to shatter to pieces when the legs are given a sharp tap. Similarly, suppose you know that the chair has been painted with an unusual shellac that triggers allergic reactions among a large proportion of people. While the chair may appear ordinary at first glance, it may in fact be unsuitable as func-tional furniture—which makes it different from what is understood by "ordinary wooden chair." In these situations, where you know that the chair has risks that set it apart from conventional "ordinary chairs," you have to explain these risks to Peter Piper.

Notice that there are a host of topics that you may or may not decide to disclose about the chair. In fact, it may be good business and in your own rational self-interest to disclose a lot about the chair you are trying to sell. If you generally disclose a great deal to your potential trading partners it may boost your good reputation as a trustworthy, informative business professional. For example, you may decide to announce who designed and made the chair, exactly what type of wood was used, or where you obtained it.

Alternatively, you may decide not to talk about the designer, the wood, and how you came to possess the chair. This is acceptable providing you take care to avoid giving your potential buyers false impressions.

Honest Advertising

In the broadest, most general sense, advertising is your way of telling the outside world about your product or service. The purpose of advertising is to communicate what you have to offer in a persuasive manner—to put the attributes of what you are selling in an attractive, favorable, compelling light.

When advertising is done well it has value for both the seller and the buyer. To the seller it presents an argument for buying the product or service. To the buyer it summarizes the seller's pitch for buying, or to consider buying.

Good advertising is effective in catching the positive attention of the potential buyer, tells her the seller's story, and gives her an indication of how the product or service can be valuable. The potential buyer might be persuaded to investigate further and become an actual buyer. Similarly, she might be convinced to continue buying the product she has purchased previously. Of course, advertising is not always effective. Potential buyers may fail to get the message, may ignore it, or may interpret the message correctly but still reject the argument.

The principle of Acting Honestly implies that—whatever the medium, technique, or execution—advertising should depict the product or service accurately and should not mislead members of the target audience. You have to exert efforts to assure that your audience is likely to understand your story and unlikely to misinterpret it.

This is not to say that advertising ought to consist of nothing more than the dry recitation of facts. To the contrary, creative advertising might be crafted to be attention-grabbing, startling, interesting, intriguing, provocative, entertaining, wry, amusing, or funny. The rule is that among all the other ways your advertising impacts your audience, it must be fundamentally truthful—an honest portrayal that encourages an accurate understanding.

There are numerous cases where an advertisement is designed conscientiously with honest intentions, but a high proportion of people in the target audience get a wrong impression. Here it is the advertiser's responsibility to detect the error in communication and change the advertising to correct the misunderstanding.

Legalistic Misdirection

Of course there are instances where people lie—communicate in advertising, promotions, announcements, product labels, company literature—about the important attributes of products or services and say things which they know to be false. This is straight-out fraud, should not be done, and should be against the law. There is not much more to say about fraud.

More interesting than direct lies, which are relatively easy to catch, are legalistic misdirections. Here the perpetrator is careful not to say anything that is not literally true. However, he weaves the communication so that the audience is likely to form a mistaken opinion of the product or service—usually disadvantageous to the buyer.

Of course, the principle of Acting Honestly does not permit the sneaky loophole of legalistic misdirection. Your job is to say things to your audience that encourage a correct understanding. Merely refraining from direct lying does not capture the spirit of the principle. The moral precept is that you have the responsibility of communicating accurately and clearly.

Here are some common examples of attempts to mislead trading partners legalistically, without "literally lying:"

- A coffee manufacturer sells 16-ounce—that is, one-pound— cans of coffee for years. Instead of raising the price of the can, the manufacturer begins to sell a 15-ounce can of coffee— labeled correctly but designed to fool the consumer into thinking that it is the same one-pound can. The coffee manufacturer is hoping that some customers will not notice that the price of the product has surreptitiously been increased or that the amount of coffee in the package is less.

- A bank markets new credit cards that are loudly described as having "no annual fee." In fact, the cards have no annual fee only for the first year. Banking executives are expecting that many consumers will regard the credit card as attractive partly because they are mistakenly assuming there will be no fee indefinitely. The bankers intend to add a charge for the card during the second year and they are hoping that their customers will not notice, or not be bothered by, the fee.

- A general interest consumer magazine mails an offering for new subscriptions. The offering states that the subscriber will only be billed $12.95 a month for three months. Nowhere on the offering is there any explicit statement that the total cost of the subscription is $38.85. The writer of the offering is worried that the total price will appear steep to some cost-conscious consumers and wants to divert their attention. He calculates that some consumers will subscribe to the magazine partly because they think it is less expensive than it actually is.

Honesty And Greed

There is no question that Honesty is a virtue and that violating the policy of Acting Honestly is a serious transgression. However, it is important to keep the concept of Acting Honestly straight and not confuse it with virtues or vices that are unrelated.

Frequently when people in the business world are caught perpetrating the crimes of theft or fraud, commentators will automatically assert that the bad action was caused by excessive greed. When a company president is convicted of deliberately misrepresenting the profits of his company in order to keep the price of the stock high, he is described as greedy. When an executive is apprehended for embezzlement, the root of the problem is frequently described as his excessive greed. Here "greed" means having high ambitions and wanting to succeed materially more than the commentator thinks is appropriate.

The solution, according to some commentators, to outrageous instances of theft or fraud is to curb everyone's greed—to put the brakes on ambition and limit how much an individual is legitimately permitted to want.

Critics who suggest that greed causes dishonesty or that greed goes hand-in-hand with dishonesty are making an error. While thieves might indeed want a lot for themselves, it is their lack of honesty—a failure to commit themselves to the policy of acting according to what is real—not their ambition that is the problem. Saying that greed and dishonesty are logically joined is a sneaky way of suggesting that ambition itself is a vice.

The nature of the mistake of uniting dishonesty with greed can be illustrated by considering an example that is outside the world of business: Munchausen Syndrome By Proxy—a horrendous action taken by a parent who secretly harms a child in order to be seen as the rescuer of the child.

This action is a terrible crime committed by a tiny fraction of parents, usually mothers, who continuously bring their child for medical attention to treat some serious problem. The child is indeed in distress, but the cause of the child's problems is that the mother deliberately and furtively injures her child. When the child is examined by medical professionals they notice that the mother appears to be deeply concerned with the child's welfare and is apparently exerting heroic efforts to see that the child's health improves. But the child does not get well, because after each treatment the mother who is guilty of

Munchausen Syndrome By Proxy injures her child again—when no one is looking—so she can again take credit for saving her offspring.

Notice that the mother with Munchausen Syndrome By Proxy is committing two serious offenses. Most important, she is injuring another human being without justification. Also significant, she is attempting to fake reality—to take credit for being a "good, responsible, caring mother" when in fact she is just the opposite.

It is not reasonable to conclude that the woman's desire to be a good mother is what motivated her to commit Munchausen Syndrome By Proxy. The sincere motivation to be an effective parent is incompatible with faking reality. If an observer were to assert that the mother's extreme, "greedy" desire to be recognized as an outstanding parent caused her to injure her child, it would be obvious that the observer is missing the point.

Returning to the world of business, it is not greed—an extremely high level of ambition—that motivates dishonesty in business. A highly ambitious man or woman of integrity knows that the genuine realization of ambition precludes faking reality. An ethical person wants to succeed for real, not as a charade. Conversely, the root problem with the liar or thief in business is the deliberate evasion of reality, the desire to victimize others, not extreme ambition.

WHAT YOU SHOULD DO

1. Define The Issue.

The first step is to define the issue. You have to specify exactly what the topic is where Acting Honestly is salient.

You are responsible for recognizing all of the important issues that impact on your business role and for being knowledgeable about each of them.

You will have to use your best judgment and good sense in compiling a list of the things you should understand well—things that are consequential to your business. It is part of your job to keep yourself informed, to know the important questions and to find the answers. The alternative to this policy is to allow yourself to become immersed in a mental fog, to evade or ignore the truth.

Broad areas where you should be knowledgeable in order to Act Honestly include:

- The various ways that your product or service has value.

- How your business activities contribute to the value of your product and service. Conversely, how your business activities might be reducing value. You should strive to understand the causes of success and failure in your business role.

- The results of your past actions. The anticipated results of your future actions.

Sometimes the issue that you identify as important to understand will be something that you intend to keep to yourself. For example, you might be evaluating techniques you use to enhance your personal productivity on the job. While it is to your advantage to know a lot about what is contributing to your own job performance, you may choose to keep this information private.

Alternatively, there will be instances where you identify issues that are for public consumption. In essence, these are all the things that you communicate to your potential and actual trading partners. This includes communications related to marketing, advertising, promoting, selling, describing, labeling, requesting, instructing, and entertaining.

Notice that the list of topics that you have an obligation to investigate is restricted to important, essential issues when you are defining issues for your own edification. However, as soon as you decide to communicate about an issue with someone else, the issue—whether important or not—automatically jumps onto your "be careful list." Anything you say to your potential trading partners has to be honest—accurate and clear. This assures that there is no loophole for scoundrels who might try to sneak through deceptive communications and attempt to excuse themselves by claiming that the topic is not really important. If the issue is important enough for you to communicate, it is important enough for you to Act Honestly.

Let us consider some examples of defining the issue to illustrate how the process works.

Think of our simple case first. Jane Doe, the brave woman who is living in isolation, has to assure that she has enough to eat. The major options open to her are gathering, hunting, and fishing for food—in the short run, and cultivating domestic plants and animals—in the longer run.

Since Jane Doe has been on the island for only a short time, one of her immediate concerns is to be able to recognize which wild plants are edible, how to prepare them for consumption, and which plants are toxic and should be avoided.

Jane realizes that the topic of recognizing edible plants and knowing what to do with them is salient to her survival and prosperity. Therefore, she puts "knowing about plants" very high on her list of things to do. She deliberately pays attention to the vegetation on the island and strives to categorize the various plants correctly as to which are nutritious and which are noxious.

Now let us consider the more complicated case. Jack Sprat owns an aspirin manufacturing company. It is essential that he understands at some reasonable level of detail the major procedures that are used in his company to assure that the manufactured aspirin is pure, uncontaminated, and is pressed into uniform tablets of 325 mg each.

Jack not only has to know these things for his own sake, but he is also going to be communicating to the outside world. For example, the packaging for his aspirins will describe the ingredients, the dosage, the uses for aspirin, as well as some warnings.

At this point Jack has defined a number of issues that he recognizes as being consequential—where Acting Honestly is vital. Some are his private business, and some he will communicate to others.

Jack understands that aspirin is generally a commodity product. It is difficult for a small manufacturer such as himself to capture the attention of aspirin buyers. As a marketing device, he is entertaining the idea of having graphics of beaches, pineapples, and palm trees on the packaging and printing the statement "Made In Hawaii" prominently.

Notice that exactly where aspirins are made within the United States is not ordinarily considered to be an interesting topic. There are many manufacturing locations that are acceptable. However, as soon as Jack Sprat elects to describe publicly that his aspirins are "Made In Hawaii" he has an obligation to Act Honestly with respect to disclosing where his product is manufactured. Jack must be accurate and clear on the topic.

2. Assess What You Know.

You should take stock of what you know about the issue. Unless the issue is very simple, it is a good idea to put your list of facts in writing. It is very easy to lose track, and writing is a useful discipline to keep you on course.

For every important conclusion make a note of your source of information. Why do you think that? What is the evidence and how reliable is it? What is your reasoning process for evaluating the evidence? Putting these questions and answers in writing makes it easier to see gaps that merit more attention on your part. Documentation is assurance against your getting lost.

Besides assessing what you know, you should also make a list of what you do not know. What is not clear to you? What should you investigate further? How can you get the required information that will assure that you Act Honestly?

Let us return to Jane Doe, the woman who is supporting herself in the wilderness. She has to be knowledgeable about what plants she can safely eat. Fortunately, Jane had the foresight to bring a survival book with her to the island. It contains a chapter that shows pictures, provides names, and presents facts about wild fruits and vegetables that are edible. The chapter also describes a number of wild vegetables that are poisonous to humans.

Jane uses her survival book as an expert source of information in classifying the flora she encounters. Jane notices that not all of the plants on her island are depicted in the book. She encounters a number of plants not mentioned in the book that look as if they could be safely consumed.

Jane knows that while the survival book gives her an advantage, it is not the final word on what to eat and what to avoid. She has to experiment with each vegetable she consumes to gain additional infor-mation. If a plant tastes terrible or makes her sick she knows to avoid it—regardless of what the book might suggest. Similarly, she will have to use her best judgment in deciding which plants to taste that are not referenced in her survival book.

Because she is fastidious, Jane keeps a record of what plants she samples, how she prepares them, and the effects they seem to have on her. Her recorded notes are particularly useful since they combine the information obtained from the survival book with her personal experiences.

What about Jack Sprat, the owner of the aspirin manufacturing company? If he wants to imprint "Made In Hawaii" on his aspirin packages, he has to be certain that he has his facts straight. Because he has decided to communicate about where his aspirins are made, he is obligated to be well-versed on the subject.

Are Jack Sprat's aspirins actually manufactured in Hawaii or are they manufactured elsewhere and then packaged in Hawaii? "Made In Hawaii" suggests that they are both manufactured and—unless something else is written on the package to the contrary—packaged in that state. The declaration probably suggests nothing about where the aspirin bottles and cardboard packages were made.

Jack does his homework and carefully investigates how his aspirins are made, packaged, and transported to his customers. Furthermore, he frequently updates this information and keeps it in his company's records.

3. Devise A Communication Strategy.

You have to assert what you have good reasons to believe is true and memorialize it.

If the issue is private and for yourself alone, at a minimum you should verbalize your conclusions to make them stick. Better than relying on your personal oral tradition, where mistakes and lapses of memory can easily occur, is to put the main points in writing. Keep a journal "for your eyes only" of what you are thinking and how you are dealing with important issues.

When you are communicating with someone else, your goal is to be accurate and clear. Your task is to convey information to your intended audience. Notice that this is different from leaving clues that could be picked up by an astute detective. Once you decide to say anything, you do not want to obscure your message in "fine print" or in a sea of extraneous assertions. Do not repeat the error of the coffee manufacturer who disguises a 15-ounce can to resemble a 16-ounce, one full pound, can of coffee.

Jane Doe, who needs to Act Honestly with respect to classifying vegetables as edible or poisonous, keeps notes for herself documenting her experiences. Her notes are mental artifacts that permit her to record a lot of pertinent information which she can easily retrieve anytime in the future. Because she keeps a written record, Jane does not have to get into the ritual of verbally repeating her discoveries about vegetables. Since she can always go back and read her notes, she is free to turn her attention to other important matters.

Jack Sprat intends to use "Made In Hawaii" as a marketing technique that he hopes will get the attention of purchasing managers and of consumers who use aspirin. Jack has to consider what color scheme, typeface, and print size will best convey his message. Furthermore, he has to weigh how, if at all, "Made In Hawaii" should be a part of his advertising and promotion that goes beyond package design. Jack becomes involved in selecting beach, pineapple, and palm tree graphics that effectively inform his target audience.

Jack must take seriously the objective that his intended audience will understand that his aspirins are made in Hawaii. Of course, this is not all that Jack hopes to achieve. He is calculating that "Made In Hawaii" will get the attention of potential buyers who will then investigate further. Once they look into his product they will discover that there are tangible reasons for preferring it—including an ergonomic bottle, tablets that are specially shaped to be easy to swallow, and a prominent, legibly printed expiration date.

Jack knows that while it is important that his communications are persuasive, the principle of Act Honestly implies that it is essential that what he says is accurate and clear.

4. Test Your Effectiveness.

You should always go back and check how well you are Acting Honestly. This means that you should assess the quality of the information you are obtaining for yourself and the extent to which you are effectively communicating with others. When you learn that you are doing a good job, you should be pleased. Alternatively, if you discover that you are not being effective, you have a cue to take corrective actions.

It is a mistake to skip this self-checking step. If you do not deliberately assess how well you are doing it is easy to lose track, to drift off course, to be unaware of the degree to which you are Acting Honestly.

If the issue is a private matter, for your eyes only, you should review what you know and how you are acting on this knowledge. You have to be honest with yourself about personal issues that are consequential, issues that impact on how well you are doing your job.

When the issue is something that you are communicating to others, you have to be especially careful that you are accurate and clear. A scoundrel might skip this step, hoping that the audience will misunderstand—might have an inflated idea of the product or service or might miss some value-reducing danger that is hidden in the "fine print."

Take note that when you are sending messages to others, while you should strive to be understood, you are not in a position to guarantee that everyone will comprehend you. There will almost always be some people who simply do not grasp—sometimes intentionally—what you are trying to tell them. This means that, realistically, your task in Acting Honestly is to go with the communication that is most likely to be understood. For example, in deciding between any two executions of a true message—whether they are letters, labels, advertisements, appeals, slogans, announcements, or instructions—you should favor the execution that is more likely to be correctly comprehended.

Let us go back to Jane Doe, who needs to classify wild plants as being either edible or poisonous. She is keeping a written record of what plants she encounters on her island and her experiences with them. Jane has to go back to her written notes and test how well they are informing her.

Jane will know that she is doing a good job if she finds that her notes are useful, that she is consistently able to differentiate the plants on the island accurately, and that as she makes more entries in her journal her life gets easier and she prospers. If she accomplishes this she has concrete, specific evidence that she is Acting Honestly and that her method is paying off.

However, Jane might find that her observations were done in a careless manner, that her handwriting is illegible, that her notes are too cryptic, or that the paper she is using is rapidly deteriorating. If these circumstances occur, Jane will know that she has to fix what is broken—has to devise a better system of keeping herself informed as to the nature of the plants on the island.

Jack Sprat has to assure himself that the "Made In Hawaii" aspirin package is accurate and clear. At a minimum he should scrutinize the label by himself and verify that it says exactly what it is supposed to say and does not imply anything that is not true.

In an effort to catch accidental errors Jack asks some of the employees in his aspirin company to examine the "Made In Hawaii" label. What is the label saying to you? What is it making you think about the aspirins? Aside from how interesting or compelling the label appears to Jack's employees, the important issue is that the label communicates where the aspirins are made and does not suggest anything that is false. To Jack's satisfaction, the employees who study the proposed label uniformly play back the intended message.

At this point Jack has completed the requirements for testing his communication. He is saying something about his aspirins that is true, and he has reasons to believe that the communication is clear.

While he is not obligated to do so, Jack decides to go further before he finalizes the label. He elects to do some formal marketing research—spending time and money to get a measure of how people outside of his company—retail executives and consumers—interpret the label.

He hires a marketing research company to show the aspirin labels to a sample of people who would be his potential customers—purchasing agents for retail establishments and consumers who routinely buy aspirin. The results of the research indicate that the message "Made In Hawaii" is understood by virtually all of the people in the target audience. However, a sizable proportion of consumers look at the label and interpret the graphic of the pineapple to suggest that the aspirins contain ingredients derived from pineapples.

Now Jack has information that motivates him to change the package design of the aspirins. In fact, he never meant to say that his aspirins are made from pineapples, and a careful inspection of the label does not imply to an informed reader that any tropical fruit derivatives are added to his product. However, Jack has evidence that a significant number of consumers—who are his potential customers—will get the wrong impression from his product label.

To remedy the situation Jack tests a new package design—similar to the original version but omitting the pineapple graphic. When he does another round of marketing research he discovers that consumers are more likely to interpret the modified design accurately. Jack now knows that his package communicates more effectively if there is no picture of a pineapple.

Notice that Jack attempts to create a package design that describes his product clearly. But "clearly" does not mean that all consumers under all circumstances will get the message. No matter what Jack puts on his product label there will inevitably be some consumers who will fail to get it right. Jack is acting properly when he adheres to the policy of preferring the package design that is more likely to be understood correctly by a reasonable person.

9

DEAL BY MUTUAL CONSENT

HOW TO THINK ABOUT MUTUAL CONSENT

Mutual Consent—Recognizing Rights

Dealing voluntarily by Mutual Consent means that both you and your trading partner affiliate with one another only when each of you is acting by your own free will, not under coercion. When you earnestly embrace this principle you are demonstrating your respect for each individual's rights.

The negative way to state this rule is that it is not ethical to initiate force when you do business. Using force to achieve business objectives is not compatible with acting morally.

Notice that there are two fundamental, mutually exclusive choices. You can deal with others by voluntary Mutual Consent or by coercive force.

Dealing by Mutual Consent means that you must use persuasion to convince your potential trading partner to do business with you. When the ground rule is Mutual Consent you are counting on your own, and your potential trading partner's, rationality to reach an acceptable agreement. Whatever you want from your trading partner, the proper way to get it is through persuasive arguments. This might consist of having conversations, sending messages, advertising, or establishing your reputation to the world at large.

The recipients of your persuasion attempts have the option of accepting your pitch and deciding to trade with you. They also have the option of rejecting your proposal for doing business—possibly for intelligent reasons, possibly because they misunderstand your business proposition, or possibly for no good rationale at all.

In sharp contrast to adhering to the principle of Mutual Consent, when someone deals with others and resorts to initiating physical force, the virtue of rationality is desecrated. People who deal with others by initiating physical force are explicitly violating others' rights to their own lives. Employing force, or threatening force—"do what I demand or else," depends upon the other person's fear of getting harmed. Anyone using this tactic has abandoned the idea that trading should appeal to each person's reason and self-interest. Properly speaking, business transactions where physical force is used are not genuine trades, they are coerced takings.

The Problem With Force

The conventional explanation for making the initiation of force out-of-bounds is that using force will damage your reputation. If you force or threaten people they will view you with antipathy, they will attempt to avoid you, and eventually they will retaliate against you with force. Therefore, according to the established view, you are best served by dealing only by Mutual Consent. If you are considerate of others they will be encouraged to reciprocate.

While the conventional reprimand against initiating force correctly identifies the probable consequences of being a bully, it does not name the essential reason for not initiating force. If it were only your reputation that were at stake you might incorrectly conclude that when you are stronger—or more politically powerful—than your trading partners, you can bulldoze over them with impunity. You might decide that your reputation is not so important. Who cares what your weak victims are thinking? You might as well grab everything that you can.

The fundamental reason why it is wrong to deal with people by initiating force is that it violates their natural rights to their lives.

Each person has legitimate ownership of his or her life and property. This implies that nobody can justifiably force someone else to trade. In fact, the concept of free trade implies that force is not used.

Trading by Mutual Consent is conducive to Creating Value. It permits and encourages—but does not guarantee—that each person acts according to his or her best judgment. When someone initiates force in a business situation the good judgment of the forced person is irrelevant. The victim has to comply with the bully to avoid being hurt.

Foolish Choices

When people are free to deal with one another on a strictly voluntary basis they will inevitably make some mistakes. I might accept a job that turns out to be disadvantageous to me. I might buy office equipment and later learn that it is inferior to alternative merchandise I decided not to buy. I might fail to recognize that I can get superior financial services by staying with my current bank instead of switching to a different institution.

If I am alert and paying attention to my business activities I will come to recognize my mistakes, and I will learn to make better decisions. But since I cannot be forced—and I have free will—it is possible that I will frequently make foolish choices. If I am reasonably diligent I will improve over time. Alternatively, I may be chronically foolish and fail to become a better decision-maker.

Of course, striving to make your decisions rationally—basing your actions on good reasoning—is a virtue. The morality of Radical Capitalist ethics is grounded in rationality. You and your trading partners ought to come to agreements after each of you has intelligently considered the merits of dealing or not dealing with one another. However, if your potential trading partner makes foolish choices you do not have a right to "force better choices." Similarly, no one who fails to convince you to trade has the right to force themselves upon you.

A consequence of taking the principle of personal freedom and Mutual Consent seriously is that there will always be some people who make decisions capriciously—without adequate justification. In a free society you may speak to your neighbors, furnish them with information and advice, and attempt to persuade them to do business with you. But you may not justifiably coerce them to achieve your aims. Each person has final authority over his or her own life.

The Permanent Risk Of Failure

Be aware that an implication of dealing only by Mutual Consent is that you are permanently at risk to fail. Things might not turn out the way you want. Your proposal to do business may not be acceptable to your potential trading partners. Since you cannot coerce others, they are free to decide against doing business with you.

This permanent risk of failure is particularly offensive to interventionists who oppose Capitalism. In fact, one of the interventionists' favorite arguments against Capitalism is that there are no assurances that everyone will get what the interventionist wants them to get. These power-craving meddlers cannot abide by the possibility that, as a result of individuals exercising their right to act freely in their own rational self-interest, the outcome may not turn out exactly to the interventionists' liking. The foes of Capitalism attempt to take command of the economic and political system to assure that people are compelled to comply, rather than being free to act autonomously.

Parenthetically, it is interesting to note that in command economies—where communist, socialist or "mixed economy" governments routinely give orders and make no pretense of honoring the principle of Mutual Consent—social planners still do not obtain the results that they want. The governments of non-capitalist societies are notorious for failing to achieve their objectives by brute force—and deservedly so.

The Meaning Of "Force"

Having a clear understanding of what counts as coercive force and what does not is crucial. A fairly large proportion of people are sympathetic with the principle that voluntary Mutual Consent is the right way to deal with people and that the initiation of force is wrong. But many people who work in the business world—or observe it from the outside—have difficulty distinguishing the depraved application of physical force from non-coercive attempts at persuasion.

A person is initiating force if he or she physically violates—or threatens to violate—someone else's person or property. This includes activities such as murder, assault, theft, imprisonment, detention, trespassing, vandalism, and arson. Force always involves an active move—an invasion into someone else's life—on the part of the perpetrator.

By contrast, persuading and bargaining—such as offering attractive incentives or threatening not to trade with someone—does not constitute the use of force. You may admire or condemn someone's attempts at persuasion, but you should not confuse persuasion with coercion.

Take note that in conventional parlance it is common for people to speak of attempts at persuasion by offering positive incentives as being equivalent to using force. You should learn to recognize these errors.

Here are a few examples of attempts at persuasion based on positive incentives being confused with force:

- Employees sometimes say they are "chained to their jobs with golden handcuffs." Their company is paying them more than they believe they can get elsewhere, and they "feel coerced" into staying on the job.

  Of course, in this type of situation, there is no initiation of force on the part of the company. If, alternatively, the employees were threatened with physical harm if they were to leave their jobs, then they would be right to label the company policies as coercive.

- Consumers who say they are "forced to buy" certain branded products because the products are so much cheaper than alternative products they would rather have. In a similar way consumers sometimes say they are "forced" to give up certain luxuries because the prices of premium goods are too high.

Really forcing consumers to buy particular products would consist of someone threatening to injure them unless they complied. Force is not an issue just because a buyer, or outside observer, would like to see prices lower than they are.

- Sometimes retail store owners complain that they are "forced out of business" because a large chain store offers to buy their business at a price that will give them more money than what they think they would make by staying independent. Alternatively, they might say that the chain store is "forcing" them to lower their prices—decreasing their profits—because the chain store sells merchandise for less.

  Genuine coercive force would be used if the chain store representatives threatened to take property physically or to assault the retail store owners.

Keep in mind that a legitimate trade has got to be agreeable to both parties. Consequently, it is always permissible for a potential trading partner to decide not to trade because the terms of the deal are not satisfactory. Again, it is common for people to mistake a business person's unwillingness to trade as being equivalent to using or threatening force.

Here are some examples of deciding not to trade that are sometimes confused with force:

- Employers who claim their employees "forced" them to offer a generous benefits package. Otherwise, the employees would resign and go to other companies.

  Force would be applicable if the employer were required to provide a particular benefits package on penalty of fine or imprisonment if he or she did not comply. In fact, governmental agencies commonly do force employers to implement particular benefits policies. However, when an employee threatens to quit this does not count as force.

- Food manufacturers who say that supermarkets "force" them to pay stocking fees. Otherwise the supermarket would not give the manufacturers shelf space.

  The supermarket executives are within their rights to request fees for stocking particular products. The genuine use of force would require that the supermarket executives menace the food manufacturers with things such as bodily harm, theft, or vandalism.

- Supermarket executives who say that manufacturers "force" them to stock low volume products—for example mustache wax—as a condition for providing them with more popular products that are easy for the supermarkets to sell—for example shaving cream. If the supermarket executive were to refuse the manufacturer's request to stock mustache wax, he might receive less of the popular product—shaving cream—than he wants.

  In fact the manufacturer might be a hard bargainer, but he is not using coercive force. When two parties get together to agree on a deal, either may decide that the conditions are not acceptable. If the manufacturer were to threaten to trash the supermarket if the mustache wax was not stocked, that would count as coercive force.

Why Force And Persuasion Are Confused

The delusion that force and voluntary bargaining are "really the same thing" is pervasive. You hear it from teachers—in elementary schools, high schools, colleges, and graduate schools. Journalists in print, radio, and television are frequently likening voluntary Mutual Consent in business to the coercive use of force. The world of business—claim the enemies of Capitalism—is inherently a nasty, cruel environment. Employees are often described as "wage slaves." Corporations are characterized as "manipulating" what people want and giving them no alternative other than to comply and buy products.

Many people hear the platitude that voluntary business negotiations are no different in principle from coercive force so many times, from so many commentators, that they tacitly accept the idea without critically examining it. Probably most people who blend the two incompatible concepts together are making an innocent error. They have heard a mistaken idea endlessly repeated from a wide range of sources, and they do not think to question it. Of course, it is interesting to note that given the choice nearly everyone would rather be persuaded than forced. Almost no one is indifferent to the prospect of being offered positive incentives compared to being threatened with physical coercion.

Those "intellectuals" who fashion and perpetuate the false doctrine that voluntary Mutual Consent is no different from coercive force do not have innocent motives. Their intention is to destroy the concept of Mutual Consent. When they attempt to scramble the idea of consensual negotiations with the brutal impulse to use force, they aim to confuse their audience into believing that coercion and "ordinary business practices" are essentially the same. They hope to smear the idea of trading by Mutual Consent by asserting it is essentially "equivalent to" dealing with someone at the point of a gun.

Notice that when someone intimates that force and voluntary Mutual Consent amount to the same thing, that person inevitably endorses the use of coercive force. In any given situation, someone who insists that Mutual Consent and coercive force are equivalent will go on to say that people are not capable of coming to the right solution on their own, and they have to be "compelled" to act properly. Since all human action is really forced anyway, argues the knave, it is practical to dispense with the pretense that people should be free and simply command them to obey.

Using A Surrogate Enforcer

Your business dealings are ethically proper only if they occur by Mutual Consent. It is not permissible for you to force someone else to do business or to refrain from doing business, and—reciprocally—it is not right for anyone else to force you either to do business or to stay out of a business. This rule cannot be escaped by using a surrogate enforcer.

Sometimes villains attempt to get around the prohibition against initiating force by using a surrogate. They hope to keep their own hands clean and hire thugs to do their dirty work—harming or threatening to harm others. This vile tactic is familiar to anyone who has read stories or seen movies about gangsters. The big boss typically does not commit violence himself, but he sends his hoodlums out to intimidate his intended victims into compliance.

It should not be difficult to understand that even as it is wrong to initiate force or to menace others when you are doing business, it is also reprehensible to engage someone else to commit offenses on your behalf.

But what if that someone else is the government? Is it acceptable to use government muscle to intimidate others into dealing with you on your terms? The short answer is no.

Government is a vital and necessary element in a Radical Capitalist society. It has a monopoly on the legal use of retaliatory physical force—under the control of objectively defined laws. The proper function of government is limited to the protection of each individual's rights—to life, liberty, and property.

In today's world there are numerous instances where governmental policies and actions with respect to business are entirely appropriate—where the government uses its power to assure that the initiation of force or the use of fraud is not tolerated or permitted. Unfortunately, there are also occasions where the authority of the state is hijacked by unscrupulous persons who use government muscle to force outcomes they could not achieve through voluntary consent. In essence these miscreants have learned to abuse the political system and use the government to take what they want.

Some examples of debasing the legitimate role of government:

- A small town has an independently-owned restaurant special-izing in roasted chicken and the proprietor is well-known in the local community. A national company that has a large chain of roasted chicken outlets opens a competing store nearby. The owner knows that the chain store will be likely to attract some of his customers. He goes to the town govern-ment and requests a zoning ordinance that will compel the national company to close its operations in the town. The rationale is that the small town is only large enough to support one specialty chicken restaurant—the one that got to the town first.

  Notice that the independent proprietor chose to use force, by way of government power, to block the national chain from doing business in his town. He had the option of competing openly and honestly against the chain. For example, he might have positioned his roasted chicken as fresher, prepared locally, seasoned with higher-quality ingredients, or unique because he uses a recipe that is special to the geograph-ical region. These business tactics may be effective and do not violate the principle of Mutual Consent.

- The management of a national company that has a large chain of roasted chicken restaurants is thinking of opening a new store in a small town that presently has only one independ-ently-owned restaurant, specializing in roasted chicken. The managers of the national chain believe they have found an "ideal location" on the Main Street of the town where traffic is high and potential customers are plentiful. The "ideal loca-tion" is currently occupied by an antiques store. The owner of the antiques store is offered a substantial sum of money by the national company for his site, but he does not want to sell.

To achieve their business goals, representatives of the national company go to the town government and suggest that the town use eminent domain to condemn the antiques store, pay the owner a "fair price" which will come from the national company, and permit the national company to open a chicken restaurant on the site. The national company executives argue that their restaurant will employ more people than the antiques store, will generate more tax dollars for the local government, and will result in added prosperity for the town.

The national company executives are guilty of initiating force against the owner of the antiques store. They have legitimate options—offer him more money, find an alternative location within the town, do not open any store in the town. As soon as they talk about using the power of eminent domain with the town government they have stepped over the line and are violating a key ethical principle—respect each person's right to life and property.

- In an East Coast State with a substantial dairy industry, many of the dairy farmers find that they cannot sell milk as profitably as they would like. Distributors and retail outlets within the state are getting good deals on milk from farmers who are producing dairy products in neighboring states. In essence the dairy farmers are competing against out-of-state low-cost producers. The East Coast State dairy farmer association goes to the state legislature and lobbies for the passage of a law that would put a minimum price on what distributors and retailers would have to pay for milk. The new law would make it illegal for milk sellers to attempt to get better deals from out-of-state vendors than they can obtain from in-state vendors. The law is justified by its sponsors as saving the livelihood of local dairy farmers.

  Notice that this minimum price takes away by force the

ability of milk retailers and consumers to deal by Mutual Consent with vendors who are in neighboring states. It is functionally equivalent to the East Coast State farmers telling wholesale buyers at gunpoint that buyers are not allowed to deal freely with producers outside of the state.

- Due to a variety of factors—including increased production and transportation costs—the price of milk is elevated significantly in a West Coast State. Members of a political action organization become alarmed that something as important as milk is becoming more expensive. They introduce a bill to the West Coast State legislature that would put a ceiling on the price of milk that retailers can charge consumers. If the bill passes it will be against the law for stores to charge more than "the maximum amount" for milk. The proposed law is justified by the claim that it will keep milk affordable to consumers—especially those with children.

  Here the political action club members have the mistaken notion that their desire to put an upper limit on the price of milk overrules the rights of buyers and sellers to come to an agreement by Mutual Consent. Incidentally, an economist might point out correctly that the "upper limit law" will be likely to result in shortages in milk—producers and retailers will have less incentive to deliver milk to consumers. The main point in this example, however, is that the members of the political action club have no compunction about using coercive force to achieve their ends.

- The management of Sore User Systems is aware that many of its potential customers have decided not to buy its products and are, instead, purchasing from its competitor Alfalfa Mail Systems—a company that bundles a free software pack with every product it sells. Sore User Systems management does not have the resources to match its competitor's offering.

Giving away free software is judged to be too expensive. As an alternative to offering potential customers positive incentives, Sore User Systems management goes to the Federal Government and complains that it is unfair for Alfalfa Mail to bundle its two attractive products. If the Federal Government does not forcefully intervene and preclude Alfalfa Mail Systems from bundling, Sore User Systems management fears it will not be able to be profitable and may even be forced out of business. The Sore User Systems management team is pleased when they succeed in getting a government directive that forbids Alfalfa Mail Systems from giving away free software.

Here Sore User Systems executives have concluded that if they do not have the skill to succeed by ordinary economic competition, they will attempt to use government muscle to get their way. Of course, they have the moral options of improving their product offering, lowering their prices, marketing more cleverly, or getting out of the business all together. Coercive force is never a legitimate business policy. If the executives at Sore User Systems were ethical they would see that they have no right to initiate force upon their competitors, whether the force comes from themselves, a hired thug, or an agent of the government.

- Alfalfa Mail Systems has the most popular products in the United States. Competitive software suites are being produced in Europe and in Asia that are significantly less expensive. Lobbyists hired by Alfalfa Mail Systems plead with Federal agencies to put a tariff on any imported software that competes with Alfalfa products. The rationale offered by the lobbyists is that the tariff will be helpful to the domestic software industry as a whole and will assure its continued success.

The essence of the Alfalfa Mail Systems proposal will be to force, via government coercion, potential customers to pay more than they would otherwise for software that comes from Alfalfa Mail Software's foreign competitors. The lobbyists for Alfalfa Mail Systems are asking the government to use its power to prevent buyers in the United States to deal by Mutual Consent with foreign vendors.

Mutual Consent And Blackmail

Keep in mind that dealing by Mutual Consent is a necessary condition for doing business ethically. It is not, however, a sufficient condition. There are instances where individuals are not using physical coercion on one another, yet they are violating important moral principles.

The case of blackmail can be used to illustrate a class of abuses where force or threats of force are not used, but the transaction is tainted.

Suppose Robert Rodent, a character with nasty intentions, spies on Sammy Sneak and discovers that Sammy has committed some act that would greatly embarrass Sammy if others knew about it. Robert approaches Sammy and proposes a deal—Robert will not tell if Sammy pays him a sizable amount of money. Robert is now blackmailing Sammy.

It is significant that Robert does not physically harm Sammy nor does Robert make any threats of violence. Sammy may suffer terrible consequences—at the hands of other people—if Robert tells on him, but Robert's implied threat does not meet the test of forceful coercion.

Using blackmail, while not necessarily dependent on the initiation of force, is condemned by the Radical Capitalist ethics code. Consider the case where Robert has discovered that Sammy has committed a crime—for example has embezzled money from his employer. In this situation if Robert demands money for his silence, Robert is becoming an accessory to the crime. He has become Sammy's accomplice in the embezzlement.

But what is occurring if Robert is demanding money in return for keeping silent about something Sammy did that is not criminal? As an example, suppose Sammy is smoking cigarettes on the sneak long after he proclaimed to his family and friends that he had given up the habit for good. If Sammy's acquaintances were to learn about his transgression from Robert, Sammy would be humiliated.

When Robert blackmails Sammy over a non-criminal matter, Robert—while he is not threatening force—is in the wrong, and the transaction is immoral. The major problem is that Robert is violating the first principle of Radical Capitalist Ethics—Create Value. Extorting money from a victim is not delivering a valuable product or service.

Consider the dynamics of a relationship based on blackmail. From the very beginning of the exchange the person being victimized will feel intense antipathy for his or her tormenter. This feeling will not improve over time. Take note that in ordinary business situations traders will often come to like one another, will sometimes have neutral feelings, and occasionally will develop a mutual aversion. But in the blackmail paradigm, the victim will always find the blackmailer odious.

Also notice that in a proper business relationship, where Value is traded for Value, the trading partners generally believe they are better off than they would have been had they not met. If, over time, one of the traders believes he is worse off, he will terminate the trading. In the case of blackmail, however, the victim always feels worse off. Victims of blackmail, without exception, wish their tormenters would go away, or cease to exist.

Determining A Fair Price

The principle of Mutual Consent is the standard for judging the fair price for a good or a service. Whatever price is acceptable to both you and your trading partner is the fair price. While the seller might wish the price were higher and the buyer might yearn for a lower price, if the deal is made by Mutual Consent—assuming each party is trading Value for Value and Acting Honestly—the matter is settled and the price is fair.

WHAT YOU SHOULD DO

Dealing by Mutual Consent is a necessary, but not a sufficient, condition for a business relationship to be ethical. The essence of the Mutual Consent principle is the recognition that you own your life and have natural rights that derive from that ownership. In a parallel fashion your potential trading partner owns his or her life. You deal by Mutual Consent because the alternative—using coercive force—is an unjustifiable abuse against you, your trading partner, or both.

Your task is to become proficient in recognizing when trades are occurring by Mutual Consent and distinguishing these situations from instances where people are using or threatening coercive force.

When you are clear on the application of the Mutual Consent principle, you should assure that you abide by it in your own business actions and that you do not sanction violations in others.

1. List The Influence Attempts.

There are two parties involved in every deal. Whether you are an active participant or an outside observer, the first step is to identify the ways each party is attempting to influence the outcome of the deal.

Make a list of the influence attempts. You should pay attention to what is being done and what is being said by each participant. Influence attempts include actions, communications that describe the advantages and liabilities of dealing with one another, promises of future positive outcomes, and threats of future negative outcomes.

As we have done previously with Create Value and with Act Honestly, we will consider some simple examples to illustrate how to proceed. We will begin by describing conventional influencing attempts.

Consider Jane Doe, the self-sufficient woman who is living in isolation and supporting herself largely by gathering and cultivating fruits and vegetables. As long as she is all by herself, the issue of Mutual Consent does not arise.

However, one day Jane's world changes. She discovers that there is another person living near her on the island, Mary Contrary. Mary is also sustaining herself alone but has a somewhat different style. Mary is highly skilled at fishing and at preparing seafood. At any given time Mary has an abundant supply of edible fish. However, Mary is not proficient with plants and does not have many fruits or vegetables in her larder.

Jane Doe and Mary Contrary meet and discuss the topic of trading with one another.

It is possible that neither Jane nor Mary are in any mood to trade. Jane is content to live primarily on her vegetables and has no desire to add fish to her diet. Similarly, Mary enjoys her fishing lifestyle and has no interest in consuming any more vegetables than she already does. They readily agree, by Mutual Consent, to continue living as they have before they met—having no compelling reason to exchange fish or vegetables.

Another possibility is that Jane sees Mary's ample supply of fish and is salivating over the prospect of adding seafood to her diet. Jane might attempt to persuade Mary to trade in a number of legitimate ways. For example, Jane might:

- Explain to Mary that Jane's vegetables are very delicious, healthy, and valuable. She could suggest that Mary would be a much happier person if she had a reliable supply of high-quality vegetables available to her.

- Offer Mary a large amount of her vegetables in exchange for a modest number of fish. In essence Jane is attempting to sell her vegetables inexpensively—giving Mary a bargain.

- Argue that each of them would be healthier if their diets were balanced with the high protein inherent in fish and the high fiber and vitamin content of vegetables.

- Propose to work, rather than trade vegetables, in exchange for some of Mary's fish. Mary might have no interest in eating more vegetables but could use an assistant in some of her daily tasks.

Of course, it might be that Mary Contrary has a keen desire to consume some of Jane's vegetables, while Jane is cool to the idea of eating any of Mary's fish. In an attempt to influence Jane, Mary might:

- Argue that they ought to trade with one another simply because both of them are living on the same island. Even if Jane has no particular desire to increase her consumption of fish, Mary might assert that they should trade with one another to establish and maintain "friendly relations." Jane may accept or reject Mary's weak argument. It is noteworthy, however, that Mary's appeal for social solidarity does not constitute coercive force against Jane so long as it is made as a suggestion.

- Say that she really wants Jane's vegetables, even though she has nothing to trade for them that Jane wants. In essence, Mary is asking Jane to bestow a gift upon her. While Mary's begging for a handout—rather than proposing a trade— suggests that Mary is lacking in pride, there is no violation of the Mutual Consent rule so long as there is no implication that Mary will retaliate with force if she does not get her way.

Now consider some slightly more complicated examples. Recall that Jack Sprat has an aspirin company that manufactures products in Hawaii. He meets with an executive from Big Mart, a major retailing chain.

After some preliminary discussion Jack and the Big Mart executive might conclude that they have little to gain from one another. Jack thinks he can sell all the aspirins he can make without dealing with

Big Mart. Similarly, the Big Mart executive believes that there is no advantage to adding another aspirin brand to the store's product line.

Alternatively, Jack might have a strong yearning to have his products sold on Big Mart's shelves. He could make several suggestions to the Big Mart executive:

- Big Mart's customers will be pleased with the novelty of being able to buy aspirins that are made in Hawaii. Big Mart will be able to charge a premium price, and realize a substantial profit margin, if they stock Jack's aspirins.

- Because he really wants to do business with Big Mart, Jack is willing to sell his aspirins very inexpensively.

- Jack is willing to give Big Mart an exclusive agreement. Big Mart will be the only major retailer that can sell his Hawaiian-made aspirins. Furthermore, Jack plans to advertise his aspirins in various consumer magazines and will emphasize in the advertising that the product is available only at Big Mart

- Jack knows that Big Mart goes to various manufacturers to obtain private-label aspirins. The manufacturers make the product but the packaging says "Big Mart." Jack offers to become a private-label supplier.

The Big Mart executive may be interested in obtaining Jack's aspirins for Big Mart's stores. He may make the following proposals:

- Jack should, the Big Mart executive argues, do everything he can to become a Big Mart supplier. The retail chain will provide Jack with the opportunity to have his aspirins sold nationwide by a retailer that has a record of success with specialty products.

- The Big Mart executive could offer Jack an exclusive deal. Jack's aspirins will be the only non-major brand of aspirins sold at Big Mart's stores.

2. Classify Tactics Of Influence.

You have to discriminate between influence attempts that are consistent with the principle of Mutual Consent from those that are not.

For people with a sound intellectual grasp of the principle, classifying influence attempts as being either in the realm of Mutual Consent or being examples of coercive force is usually simple. As fast as the situation can be described to them, they accurately recognize the nature of the deal.

However, for a lot of people classifying is not so easy. Those who are not comfortable with the concept of Mutual Consent often have tremendous difficulty distinguishing Mutual Consent from coercive force. Sometimes they are prone to false alarms—erroneously becoming hypersensitive and labeling nearly any vigorous bargaining as constituting force. At the other extreme, people who do not understand Mutual Consent might make erroneous judgments that are false negatives—becoming desensitized to coercive tactics and failing to see violations of individual rights.

A false alarm, the error of concluding that an influence attempt is relying on force—when force is not being used—is often due to confusing methods with outcomes. The principle of Mutual Consent is concerned with method—how human beings should deal with one another. The outcome of a deal based on Mutual Consent may or may not be optimally desirable to one or both of the participants. And, of course, an outside observer may or may not be pleased with the final results of the negotiation. You have to guard against falling for the common fallacy that when someone does not get exactly what he or she wants, that person was coerced.

Let us look at some situations that might trigger false alarms. Again we will return to Jane Doe, who is supporting herself on the distant island, and Jack Sprat, who is the proprietor of an aspirin manufacturing company.

Jane Doe and Mary Contrary are having vigorous discussions about trading Jane's vegetables for Mary's fish. Mary uses a number of tactics that might be mistaken for coercive force:

- Jane threatens to have nothing to do with Mary unless Mary trades on Jane's terms. In essence Jane is giving Mary an ultimatum, do it my way or I will not talk or deal with you at all. Notice that if Jane were to carry out her ultimatum she would not interfere with Mary's life or property. Cutting off all negotiations is equivalent to putting Jane and Mary back to where they were before they met.

- Jane decides that the only way she wants to sell her vegetables to Mary is expensively. This means that Jane is asking for a large number of fish and in return is offering Mary only a few of her vegetables. Mary might mistakenly conclude that Jane is "forcing" a high price on her vegetables. But, in fact, force is not an issue at all. The proper price of Jane's vegetables is precisely that price where both Jane and Mary agree. If they cannot come to an agreement by Mutual Consent, the vegetables should not be traded.

- Jane decides to time the discussions with Mary so that they occur only when Jane thinks that Mary is hungry. Jane calculates that Mary will be a more agreeable bargaining partner if Mary is really in the mood to consume fruits and vegetables. Is Jane violating Mary's rights by deliberately timing the discussions to occasions when Mary has not eaten?

  Jane is using a bargaining tactic of negotiating when she thinks that Mary will be most likely to meet her requests. Notice that no force is being used. Mary has the option of deliberately refraining from bargaining when she is hungry. Mary could make a counter proposal that all discussions occur only when she has a full stomach.

Jack Sprat is having intense discussions with the Big Mart executive about the chain selling Jack's aspirins in its retail outlets:

- Jack explains that he believes his aspirins will sell very well—whether Big Mart buys from him or not. He tells the Big Mart executive that if they do not reach an agreement, he plans to run a number of print ads in magazines that will state that his aspirins are "not available at Big Mart." The Big Mart executive believes that Jack is making a threat—bad publicity for Big Mart if Jack does not get the deal he wants. Is Jack using unfair coercive force by announcing his advertising plans?

  Jack is not at risk for violating Mutual Consent so long as he sticks to the truth and does not suggest anything that is misleading. If, in fact, his aspirins are not available at Big Mart, he has the right to inform his potential customers.

- Jack senses that the Big Mart executive considers Jack's aspirins to be a very desirable novelty item which is likely to sell very well. Jack attempts to take advantage of this by demanding a very high price for his aspirins. Is Jack "forcing" Big Mart to pay more than it should for his aspirins?

  No matter how much Jack asks for his aspirins, the Big Mart executive always has the option of rejecting Jack's offer. Asking for a high price is a legitimate move on Jack's part and is not a violation of Mutual Consent. Of course, Jack should realize when he prices his aspirins expensively that he risks turning off the Big Mart executive and might fail to sell anything at all to the retail chain.

- The Big Mart executive tells Jack that if he wants to sell aspirins to Big Mart, Jack will have to meet Big Mart's unusual demands. Jack is asked to become a private label supplier for Big Mart. All of his aspirins will be sold under the Big Mart label. Furthermore, the Big Mart executive wants an exclusive deal and insists that Jack stop selling his aspirins to other retailers. Is Big Mart forcing—in the coercive sense—Jack into a corner from which he cannot escape?

In fact, the Big Mart request for an exclusive deal is not coercive at all. Jack can walk away from the negotiations at any time and be no worse off than if he had not met with the Big Mart executive in the first place. Jack has to evaluate the extent to which he would like to shift all of his retail business to Big Mart. However Jack decides, it will be a case of bargaining through Mutual Consent.

Now we shall turn to the other type of error that can be made in classifying influence attempts—the false negative, failing to recognize that an action is coercive.

Why do observers make this kind of mistake? You should be aware of three common causes. First, in the real world coercive force is used so often—and scoundrels get away with it so frequently—that it is possible to become insensitive and not notice it. You see coercive tactics so much that they are part of the landscape. Unfortunately, there are even instances where "forcing someone to trade" is legal and sanctioned by government authorities.

Second, some people have only a superficial understanding of the principle of Mutual Consent and do not take it seriously. They view themselves as "pragmatic" and are pleased to describe themselves as not being "ideologues"—not constrained by any "overly strict" principles. They agree that in the "ideal world"—but not in the real world—all business deals would be voluntary. However, in real life one has to do whatever it takes, and it is sometimes expedient to use force. In essence they are confused by the end-justifies-the-means fallacy. This is the mistaken notion that using force is wrong if the observer does not approve of the outcome. On the other hand, if the observer is pleased with the outcome of a bargain, any coercive tactics that were used can be discounted, forgiven, or ignored.

Third, some people—particularly those who advocate a "planned" economy and whine about "social justice"—do not accept the principle of Mutual Consent at all. A rule requiring that business deals must voluntarily be accepted by both parties removes the power of the outside meddler to determine the outcome.

Some interventionists do not have the courage to put their cards on the table—they do not want to declare brazenly—even to themselves—that they oppose Mutual Consent. They compromise by giving lip service to the notion that coercive force is wrong and then deliberately deny that force is being used when force happens to serve their purposes.

Now, let us look at some examples of situations where errors that are false negatives might occur.

Returning to Jane Doe, the skilled horticulturist, and Mary Contrary, the accomplished fish-catcher, we see that Mary uses a number of tactics that might not be recognized as being coercive:

- After pleading unsuccessfully with Jane to give her vegetables, Mary decides to sneak into Jane's garden when Jane is sleeping and take the vegetables she wants. Mary rationalizes her actions on several grounds. First, Mary has a strong craving for Jane's vegetables and feels that she really needs them. Mary reckons that her own desire for vegetables trumps Jane's rights to her own personal property. Second, Mary notes that Jane has so much produce in her garden that she will never miss the vegetables that are being stolen. Third, Mary notes that she has already attempted to bargain with Jane by Mutual Consent, and since Jane did not agree, Mary has no choice but to take whatever she wants without Jane's permission.

  Mary is wrong on every count. First, just because Mary wants vegetables does not give her the right to violate anyone else's life or property. Second, the amount of produce that

Jane owns in no way affects the fact that taking without permission constitutes stealing. It is a serious violation of individual rights to steal from anyone, whether the person has meager or substantial assets. Third, excusing coercive force on the grounds that bargaining did not work is a favorite rationalization of scoundrels. Voluntary negotiation implies that there is a possibility that you will not get what you want. Failing to get the outcome you want is not a justification for thievery.

- During the course of negotiations, Mary threatens Jane. She states that unless Jane voluntarily parts with some of her vegetables, Mary will set fire to Jane's crops. Mary feels she is warranted in making the threat because Jane had previously made a threat of her own—suggesting that she would cut off all contact with Mary.

    Mary is confusing the legitimate, non-coercive threat of breaking off relations with the criminal threat of arson. She does not understand the distinction between leaving a situation—where both parties are no worse off than if they had never met—and destroying someone else's property—where Jane is the victim of Mary's malicious action.

- Mary initiates a discussion with Jane about trading fish for vegetables. For the first time in their conversations Mary brings a spear she uses to catch fish and waves it about while they talk. At one point Mary comments that although the spear is designed to catch fish, it could be used as a formidable weapon against a person if anyone gave Mary any trouble. Mary is careful never to say directly that she intends to use the spear on Jane, and Mary has the notion that she is not really threatening force because she refrains from directly stating that she might harm Jane.

    Taken in context, Mary is threatening Jane with force. There is no alternative plausible explanation for her bringing the spear to a conversation and pointing out how lethal it can be against a human. She is rationalizing her misbehavior legalistically—imagining that if she does not spell out her threat explicitly it does not count as coercion. Mary is using the same tactic gangsters use when they make a request of their human prey and add that it would be a shame if the victim were to have an accident.

Let us see what might be happening between Jack Sprat the aspirin manufacturer and the Big Mart executive that could be judged as acceptable when in fact it is not:

- The Big Mart executive who is negotiating with Jack learns that there is a government agency that is enforcing a new "equal treatment of business customers" law. In essence the law states that companies that are selling to businesses must offer exactly the same deal to any business that might be a potential customer. The Big Mart executive knows that Jack is already selling his aspirins to other retailers, sometimes on terms that are highly advantageous to the stores. He considers telling Jack that he will go to the government agency and lodge a complaint against Jack's aspirin manufacturing company, unless Jack gives in to the Big Mart executive's terms.

  The Big Mart executive is tempted to threaten Jack with governmental action. He may be thinking that there is nothing wrong with using the government agency as a tool to furthering his business interests. After all, he might rationalize, it is legal and lots of business concerns are running to the government for this type of "assistance." But the Big Mart executive is missing an important point—using the government as a surrogate to force a potential trading partner to accept your terms is equivalent to using the coercive force yourself. Even as it would be wrong for the Big Mart executive to threaten to imprison Jack or seize Jack's property, it is equally wrong for the executive to use the government to accomplish the same deed.

- Jack learns that a government regulatory agency is prosecuting companies that are accused of violating a new "fair treatment for vendors" law. In essence this law demands that large retailers, especially those in the Big Mart category, give all potential vendors a "reasonable chance." The definition of "reasonable chance" is vague enough to worry executives in large retail establishments and to encourage unscrupulous vendors and their lawyers to consider using these new laws as bargaining tools when they negotiate with retailers. Jack knows that he can go to the government agency and file a formal complaint against Big Mart—asserting that the huge retail company is in some way not giving him a "reasonable chance."

    Jack considers threatening Big Mart by saying that if his aspirins are not purchased on his terms, Jack will be inclined to register a complaint with the government regulatory agency. If Jack were to go to the government, he would be doing what a large number of other vendors have done. It is a legal maneuver and there are government officials who are urging citizens to take advantage of the "fair treatment for vendors" law. Of course, the law gives the government the power to impose fines on Big Mart—to forcefully take away its property.

    Some of Jack's acquaintances tell Jack that his going to the government does not constitute the initiation of force. It would be wrong, they argue, for Big Mart to use the government to get its way with Jack. But that is because Big Mart is large and Jack is a small operator. They contend that if the little guy uses government muscle as his means of coercion, it does not count as a violation of rights. Of course, Jack's unprincipled acquaintances are mistaken. The crime of using coercive force as a business tactic is wrong regardless of the size of the perpetrator or the size of the victim.

3. Purge Coercive Tactics.

Dealing by Mutual Consent is a necessary condition for ethical business practices. If coercive force is used in the business setting, there is always an unjustified violation of individual rights.

Once you can recognize when coercive force is occurring you should purge it from your business life. This means keeping yourself clean and encouraging proper actions in others. Doing this consists of an easy part and a difficult part.

The easy part is making certain your own actions are on track. You can decide to deal with others only by Mutual Consent—to refrain from using force in your business dealings. Here the outlook for your success is very high. You have an understanding of the rules; you control your own behavior; you make sure your conduct is proper.

The difficult part concerns how to react when other people do not respect Mutual Consent. When rascals initiate or threaten the use of coercion in business they may or may not understand the implications of what they are doing. Their actions may or may not be against the law. Attempting to correct the actions of thugs may or may not put you in personal danger.

While you do not have a positive obligation to enforce the rules of ethics in others, you should take care not to sanction the immoral behavior of initiating force. Here "sanction" means giving any kind of tacit approval. To the extent that you are able to do so, you should make it known that you support the principle of Mutual Consent and do not endorse the violation of individual rights.

Of course, you have to decide for yourself how far you will go to make your attitude known. If a brigand runs into your house toting a gun and demands your money, it may be too risky either to resist physically or to deliver a speech on appropriate ethical behavior. But at a minimum you do not sanction the brigand's action—you do not suggest that what he is doing is acceptable to you.

Let us consider some examples of how someone might respond when the principle of Mutual Consent is being violated:

- Jane Doe the expert gardener is being menaced by Mary Contrary the accomplished fisher. Mary is brandishing a spear in a threatening manner while she is asking Jane for vegetables. Jane recognizes that she is in a potentially dangerous situation. She knows that confronting Mary verbally might push Mary over the edge—resulting in a violent attack. However, Jane calculates that Mary—who has turned her back on reason—can be persuaded to come to her senses. Jane explains to Mary that violence is outside the bounds of civilized discourse, that violence is only justified by self-defense, and that using it will result in the permanent end to congenial relations.

  Will Jane's appeal to Mary's good sense succeed? There is no guarantee. Mary has free will and is responsible for whatever course she decides to take. Jane is not obligated to be bold—she would have been acting in an acceptable manner had she run from Mary. But Jane is resolved to say what she knows is right—even at the risk of her personal safety.

- Jack the owner of the aspirin manufacturing company is being threatened by the Big Mart executive. The executive tells Jack that Big Mart lawyers will file a complaint against him under the "equal treatment of business customers" law which might result in sizable fines—unless Jack complies with Big Mart's terms. Jack knows that whether Big Mart's complaint against him succeeds or not, it will be expensive for Jack to defend himself.

  Jack elects to take the high road. He tells the Big Mart executive that it is immoral to use force in business negotiations, even if it is technically legal to do so. Jack points out that he would not even consider going to the government and using the "fair treatment for vendors" law against Big Mart, because he knows it is wrong. Finally, Jack states that they should continue their negotiations—and should adhere to the rule that all bargaining is done without coercion, by Mutual Consent.

What effect will Jack's response have on the Big Mart executive? Of course, the executive has the option of carrying out his threat and seeking to gain an advantage for his company through government muscle. Alternatively, the executive might come to appreciate that coercive force has no legitimate place in business, and he might act accordingly. In either case, Jack takes a stand—does not sanction unethical action—and displays courage by defending the principle of Mutual Consent.

10

CONCLUDING COMMENT

I have presented a framework for thinking about and acting on business ethics. I will count my efforts as successful to the extent that you find it easier to come to correct conclusions and to take measures that keep you on the right moral path. If you become inspired to explain the essential virtues of Radical Capitalism to others, all the better.

Applying the principles described in this book requires your thoughtful attention. It is not an automatic, rote task like following a recipe in a cookbook. Even though you know what the topics are—Create Value, Act Honestly, Deal By Mutual Consent—you have to evaluate the available evidence, identify what is important, and use your best judgment in every instance. The task of recognizing what is ethical and acting accordingly is a lifetime endeavor.

Following is a chart that summarizes the method discussed in this book for assuring your business life is conducted ethically. Use it as a tool for focusing your attention and as a reminder that moral action, properly understood, is the way to business success.

Steps for Assuring Your Business Actions Are Ethical

Principle	What You Should Do	Done (✔)
Create Value	1. Identify Your Business Role.	
	2. Define The Product Or Service.	
	3. See How Your Role Fits.	
	4. Articulate What Is Valuable.	
	5. Consider The Downsides.	
	6. Calculate The Net Value.	
Act Honestly	1. Define The Issue.	
	2. Assess What You Know.	
	3. Devise A Communication Strategy.	
	4. Test Your Effectiveness.	
Deal By Mutual Consent	1. List The Influence Attempts.	
	2. Classify Tactics Of Influence.	
	3. Purge Coercive Tactics.	

About The Author

Barry A. Liebling is the president of Liebling Associates Corporation in New York—a boutique management consulting firm specializing in marketing, marketing research, and organizational analysis. He has spent more than two decades working with clients in advertising, consumer products, healthcare, pharmaceuticals, technology, publishing, and financial services. Liebling has a BA degree from UCLA and a PhD in psychology from Columbia University.

ORDER FORM

Think and Act on Business Ethics: A Radical Capitalist View

Purchase directly—shipped only to U.S. addresses.

Buy the book on the internet or by telephone:

Go to the website—AlertMindPublishing.com for details.

Call toll-free (800) 371-2468.

Buy the book by conventional mail:

Alert Mind Publishing. Box 8073 FDR Station. New York, NY 10150.

 $20 per book for 1, 2, 3, or 4 copies.

 $19 per book for 5, 6, 7, 8, or 9 copies.

 $18 per book for 10 or more copies.

Shipping is fixed at $5 per order, regardless of the number of books.

Sales tax is required for deliveries to New York State.

Please send me _____ book(s) @ $_____ for a total of $_____

Shipping. $ 5.00

Sales tax for New York State delivery. $_____

Total due: $_____

Make check payable to: Alert Mind Publishing.

Credit Card: ☐ American Express ☐ Discover ☐ MasterCard ☐ Visa

Number on card: _____

Expiration date: _____

Name: _____

Company (if applicable): _____

Address: _____

City: _____ State: _____ Zip: _____

Telephone: _____ E-mail Address: _____